This Day Is The Lord's

BY CORRIE TEN BOOM WITH JAMIE BUCKINGHAM

Tramp for the Lord

BY CORRIE TEN BOOM WITH C. C. CARLSON

In My Father's House

BY CORRIE TEN BOOM WITH JOHN AND ELIZABETH SHERRILL

The Hiding Place

BY CORRIE TEN BOOM

Corrie's Christmas Memories
Corrie ten Boom's Prison Letters
He Cares, He Comforts—JESUS IS VICTOR
Prison Letters
A Tramp Finds a Home—NEW LIFE VENTURES
Don't Wrestle, Just Nestle—JESUS IS VICTOR

This Day Is The Lord's

Corrie ten Boom

HODDER AND STOUGHTON
LONDON SYDNEY AUCKLAND TORONTO

Unless otherwise identified, Scripture quotations in this volume are from the King James Version of the Bible.

Scripture quotations identified LB are from The Living Bible, Copyright © 1971 by Tyndal House Publishers, Wheaton, Illinois 60187. All rights reserved.

Scripture quotations identified NEB are from The New English Bible. © The Delegates of the Oxford University Press and the Syndics of the Cambridge University Press 1961 and 1970. Reprinted by permission.

Scripture quotations identified NIV are from HOLY BIBLE, New International Version, copyright © New York International Bible Society, 1978. Used by permission of Hodder and Stoughton Ltd.

Scripture quotations identified PHILLIPS are from THE NEW TESTAMENT IN MODERN ENGLISH (Revised Edition), translated by J. B. Phillips. © J. B. Phillips 1958, 1960, 1972. Used by permission of Macmillan Publishing Co., Inc.

Scripture quotations identified RSV are from the Revised Standard Version of the Bible, copyright 1946, 1952, © 1971 and 1973.

Scripture quotations identified JERUSALEM are from The Jerusalem Bible, copyright © 1966 by Darton, Longman & Todd, Ltd., and Doubleday and Company, Inc. Used by permission of the publishers.

Scripture quotations identified NAS are from the New American Standard Bible, Copyright © THE LOCKMAN FOUNDATION 1960, 1962, 1963, 1968, 1971, 1972, 1973, 1975 and are used by permission.

Scripture quotations identifed TEV are from Good News for Modern Man—New Testament: Copyright © American Bible Society 1966, 1971, 1976.

British Library Cataloguing in Publication Data

Ten Boom, Corrie
  This day is the Lord's.
  1. Devotional calendars
  I. Title
  242'.2   BV4810

  ISBN 0–340–27158–2

Printed in Great Britain for Hodder and Stoughton Ltd., Mill Road, Dunton Green, Sevenoaks, Kent by Richard Clay Ltd., Bungay, Suffolk.

FOREWORD

Sensing the need for a new book of devotions, Corrie ten Boom began to prepare the manuscript for this book. From previously unpublished manuscripts, from copies of her letters, from tapes of her messages, and from her own daily diaries and notebooks, the manuscript for *This Day Is the Lord's*, began to take shape. She put together a brief message, a Scripture text, and a prayer for each day—day after day—until 110 days, approximately one-third of the manuscript was completed.

In August 1978, Corrie was taken with a severe stroke. She continues to be lifted up to the Lord in prayer by her loved ones and friends, by her readers everywhere, by church congregations, and by thousands attending conferences and conventions. Indeed thousands are petitioning God to touch Corrie ten Boom with His healing hand.

Corrie and her associates, Pamela Rosewell and Lotte Reimeringer, felt a burden to complete the manuscript for this book. And God helped them to do just that.

Believing that Jesus is Victor, Corrie ten Boom earnestly hopes that all who use these daily devotions will be richly blessed and that each new day the reader will be able to say "This day is the Lord's!"

JANUARY

January 1

God bless you in this new year. May He give you many opportunities to build gold and silver for eternity on the one foundation, Jesus Christ.

> Now if any one builds on the foundation with gold, silver, precious stones, wood, hay, stubble—each man's work will become manifest . . . because it will be revealed with fire . . . .
>
> 1 Corinthians 3:12, 13 RSV

With our hand in Your hand, Lord Jesus, we are more than conquerors, because Your victory is our victory. Hallelujah!

January 2

The Bible tells us that God created the earth through Jesus. He was with God when He looked at the newly created earth and said that it was very good. But then the terrible fact took place that man tore himself away from God and was sent from God's presence. The result was *sin,* misery, war, suffering, unrighteousness, death. And when God sent His Son to the earth to die for the sins of the world, very many did not accept Him. What about you? Did you accept Him as your Lord and Saviour?

Actually he (Jesus) was already in the world, because the world was created by him, and yet the world did not recognize him.

John 1:10
Parole Vivante

. . . God was in Christ, reconciling the world unto himself, not imputing their trespasses unto them. . . .

2 Corinthians 5:19

Father, we can never fully understand the wonderful oneness between You and Your Son, nor the fact that You loved us so much that You gave Your Son, that we might come back to You, and that You do not even impute our sins to us. We praise Your holy name.

January 3

When Jesus had finished all, God could bring us back to what He first made: man in His image and likeness, meant to have dominion and power over evil spirits and, above all, to have fellowship with Himself. What is our answer?

. . . put on the new nature, which is being renewed in knowledge after the image of its creator.

Colossians 3:10 RSV

Our Father, how immeasurable is Your mercy, Your lovingkindness toward us. We want to put our lives at Your disposal in a new way. Make us faithful.

January 4

God has always been seeking contact with His creation. He has not forgotten it. It was His will that man should have dominion over it, but in fellowship with Himself. Therefore, He made man in His image.

> And God said, Let us make man in our image, after our likeness: and let them have dominion. . . .
>
> Genesis 1:26

Our Father, what a wonderful calling You have for us. Forgive us that so often we marred Your image. But we thank You, that in Your Son, You made all things new—even us. Let us live our lives to Your honor.

January 5

Many people struggle with the problem of sinning and trying not to sin again. Although we know about this vicious circle of sinning and trying again and again to live up to the Christian life—and we may indeed be successful for a time—yet we fail because of our sinful nature, and the power of the enemy keeps us on the deadly treadmill of sin.

> The truth is that no condemnation now hangs over the head of those who are "in" Christ Jesus. For the new spiritual principle of life "in" Christ Jesus lifts me out of the old vicious circle of sin and death.
>
> Romans 8:1, 2 PHILLIPS

Lord, teach us what it means that, now that we are in You, we are no longer governed by our own natures. Show us the joy of surrendering to You.

January 6

Jesus came to lift us out of the vicious circle of sin and trying to live up to the Christian life, and to put us into the blessed circle of the Holy Spirit. If we then sin, we confess it immediately and are cleansed.

After confession and cleansing, we can be filled with the Holy Spirit, for there is room for Him to dwell in us. We must get into the good habit of constantly confessing our sins.

> . . . your sins are forgiven you for his name's sake.
>
> 1 John 2:12

Lord, thank You that You shed Your blood for us—for me—and that it keeps me clean from all sin.

January 7

Too often when a Christian makes a vow and fails to keep it, he explains it away as a mistake or an error of judgment. But in most cases it is not a mistake, and the vow is both valuable and possible to keep. The error is falling short of the mark.

> Thou shalt make thy prayer unto him, and he shall hear thee, and thou shalt pay thy vows.
>
> Job 22:27

Help us, Father, to obey Your command and take our vows seriously. We want to honor You.

January 8

If ever you make a foolish promise, talk it over with the Lord, but do not shrug it off. A broken vow is a sin and an affront to God. Until broken vows are mended, it is difficult to make progress on the way of consecration.

> Offer unto God thanksgiving; and pay thy vows unto the most High.
>
> Psalms 50:14

Take my will, and let it be consecrated, Lord, to Thee.

January 9

When your good is spoken evil of, your wishes are crossed, when your taste is offended, your advice disregarded, when your opinions are ridiculed and you take it all in patient, loving silence—that is victory.

> When he was reviled, he did not revile in return; when he suffered, he did not threaten; but he trusted to him who judges justly.
>
> 1 Peter 2:23 RSV

Lord, make us more like You. Help us to be victorious in the little things of everyday life.

January 10

If you are content with any food, any raiment, any climate, any society, any solitude, any interruption by the will of God—that is victory.

> . . . in any and all circumstances I have learned the secret of facing plenty and hunger, abundance and want.
>
> Philippians 4:12 RSV

Help me, Father, to examine myself closely in order to know whether I have really learned this secret. If not, please teach me.

January 11

If you never care to refer to yourself in conversation or to record your own good works—if you can truly love to be unknown—that is victory.

> For God is not so unjust as to overlook your work and the love which you showed for his sake in serving the saints, as you still do.
>
> Hebrews 6:10 RSV

Lord, help me not to look for praise or the approval of man. Let me be content with the fact that You know about what I do in serving You.

January 12

The perfect victory is to "put on the Lord Jesus Christ" and thus to triumph over one's self.

> Let Christ Jesus himself be the armour that you wear; give no more thought to satisfying the bodily appetites.
>
> Romans 13:14 NEB

Thank You, Lord, that You make us victorious in Yourself.

January 13

Often people say that one religion is as good as another. But there is a big difference between religion and Christianity. Religions tell people to try to climb from earth to heaven. Christianity is founded on Christ. He came from heaven to earth, to give eternal life to those who believe on Him.

> He that descended is the same also that ascended up far above all heavens, that he might fill all things.
>
> Ephesians 4:10

Father, thank You that You sent Your Son and that He opened up the way for us.

January 14

Religions are concerned with sins. The Bible deals with *sin*. Our Lord bore the sin of the world by identification, taking it upon Himself as if it were His own, not in sympathy. And because God had to be true to His words, Jesus had to bear the punishment for sin: death on the cross.

> . . . ye are bought with a price . . . .
>
> 1 Corinthians 6:20

How can we ever thank You, Lord, that You were willing to bear our punishment? Help us that our lives may glorify You.

Why do we long for the Lord's coming? Because we love Him. And He loves us infinitely more than we love Him. That is why I believe that He longs for that day even more than we do.

We know we must be ready at His coming—completely ready. And if we are really hoping for His return, we shall see to it that we are ready.

> And every man that hath this hope in him purifieth himself. even as he is pure.
>
> 1 John 3:3

Help us, Lord, to remember that we must daily purify ourselves. Help us to be ready for Your coming. What a joy, to see You then!

"But," you may say, "so often I try and fail. I do not succeed. However much I do my best to be pure and holy and to live in the right relationship with God and men, I deeply feel the temptations of the enemy." I believe that in these days the enemy is very, very active in attacking the children of God. He knows the time is short for him. But he is a conquered enemy.

> If any of you lack . . . let him ask God, who gives to all men generously and without reproaching, and it will be given him
>
> James 1:5 RSV

Father, You know our innermost thoughts and feelings. You know all we lack. So we come to You, asking You, and we thank You that You will give to us that which we need. With You, we will not fail.

January 17

How can you be ready? How can I be ready? Not by trying and trying again and again. That could well be a victory of pious man living a carnal life. Then we feel so good, which is a tremendous victory for the devil.

The answer is: by surrendering to Him who longs for us and who is willing to prepare us for His return.

> Because . . . you have a hope like this before you, I urge you to make certain that the day will find you at peace with God, flawless and blameless in his sight.
>
> 2 Peter 3:14 PHILLIPS

Yes, Lord, we want to surrender more fully to You. Make us willing for You to prepare us for Your return, so that we may be found ready on that wonderful day.

January 18

When we think of the last great battle, we must realize that not only the future is at stake, but that we are engaged in warfare now. We are already standing in the midst of the battle. If we have our eyes and ears open, we see how the enemy is marching in from all sides. The armor we need is not only necessary for the battle we have to fight in the future, but also for this time.

> For we are not contending against flesh and blood, but against the principalities, against the powers, against the world rulers of this present darkness . . . .
>
> Ephesians 6:12 RSV

O Lord, make us strong in the battle of today. Thank You that You are our Commander. Make us obedient to Your commands, that we may not be defeated.

January 19

God's plans for the victory are perfect. He has known the enemy and the reactions of the enemy from before the foundation of the world, and He does not need to fear any unexpected attack. At the Cross of Calvary He has already won the victory. We know our position in the battle. The Bible speaks of this position:

> . . . your life is hid with Christ in God.
>
> Colossians 3:3

Father, there is no safer position for us than to be hid with Christ in You. We thank You that it will be so in all eternity.

January 20

I am more and more impressed as I read the Bible, by the reiterated "Fear not." There are so many promises that it should not be strange if there were no "Fear not"; the promises are enough to rest upon. We should not need to be told not to be afraid, and yet there it is over and over again, in one form or another, this strong, loving, encouraging "Fear not" of our God.   AMY CARMICHAEL

> Be strong and of a good courage, fear not, nor be afraid . . .
> for the Lord thy God, he it is that doth go with thee; he will not
> fail thee, nor forsake thee.
>
> Deuteronomy 31:6

How we thank You, Father, that again and again You assure us of Your presence and that You will be with us always, to take away all our fears.

January 21

What a comfort to know that we belong to the victorious army of God, when we look at the seemingly superior forces of the enemy. Nowadays there are many atheistic ideologies. When I look at world history in the light of God's Word, then I do not believe we can expect better times. Politics has no answer for this progress of atheism.

> . . . thanks be to God, who gives us the victory through our Lord Jesus Christ.
>
> 1 Corinthians 15:57 RSV

Thank You, Father, for giving Your Son to be crucified *and* for raising Him up again. Thank You that He is alive today and that we can live in the power of His victory.

January 22

When we think of the future, when the great final battle will take place, we can very well imagine the powers of evil. But we must not forget that these are already mobilized in the battle, and it is part of our training that we recognize them and become firm.

> Submit yourselves therefore to God. Resist the devil and he will flee from you.
>
> James 4:7 RSV

Thank You, Father, that it is possible for me to be strong in Your power. Thank You that Your Word tells me so. Teach me more and more to listen to Your Word, not to the lies of the devil.

The children of God are greatly attacked at this very time, and it is good to know our enemy. That is why it is necessary to be victorious in daily life now and to surrender completely to the Lord Jesus. Jesus is always Victor! All we have to do is to remain in close contact with Him. Then His life of victory will flow through us and teach the people around us.

Our everyday life is our battlefield. Part of God's strategy is to appoint the place where we have to fight.

> . . . Your adversary the devil prowls around like a roaring lion, seeking some one to devour. Resist him, firm in your faith . . . .
>
> 1 Peter 5:8, 9 RSV

Lord, if You tell us to resist, You will also give us the power to do so. You know how much we need Your power. Thank You, that we may always ask for that which we lack.

The training in the victorious army of God for the last great battle does not take place under unusual circumstances, but in the midst of common daily life. That is the place of training, and everything we experience belongs to that training. So do our contacts with our fellow men. In Peter's first Epistle we read that all difficulties and temptations work together to prepare us:

> This means tremendous joy to you, even though at present you may be temporarily harassed by all kinds of trials. This is no accident—it happens to prove your faith, which is infinitely more valuable than gold. . . This proving of your faith is planned to result in praise and glory and honour in the day when Jesus Christ reveals himself.
>
> 1 Peter 1:6, 7 PHILLIPS

We pray, Lord, that we may be reminded of the joy that lies before us when our lives seem to be so difficult. Keep our eyes on You.

January 25

Patience is a scriptural virtue Christians must seek. There seems to be only one way, however, to gain patience, as explained in the Bible: through difficulties. You will be encouraged when you see the temptations of everyday life from God's point of view. Then you know that the greatest power of God's love and joy—the fruit of the Holy Spirit—is at your disposal in daily life.

> Count it all joy, my brethren, when you meet various trials, for you know that the testing of your faith produces steadfastness.
>
> James 1:2, 3 RSV

Lord, You alone know how much patience I need. Open my eyes when I have difficult times and trials, to help me see them from Your side and to realize that they are meant to teach me patience

January 26

What a mystery! When things are seen from the viewpoint of eternity, it makes us patient, for we know we are like gold that must be purified.

> . . . let patience have her perfect work . . . .
>
> James 1:4

Lord Jesus, thank You that You are always with me and that, when I look up, I see You. Everything else becomes small, compared to this joy.

January 27

Are you having problems in your walk as a Christian? Has sorrow come? Must you do without something or someone in order to follow Him? God has the answer. Turn to Him.

You are so much more than what you enjoy!

> But my God shall supply all your need according to his riches in glory by Christ Jesus.
>
> Philippians 4:19

Thank You, Father, for Your overflowing provision for all our needs.

January 28

The finished work at the Cross of Calvary, the power of the blood of Jesus, is our great victory. We can take this into account in our spiritual battles now and in the future. But the word of our testimony is also a power to gain the victory. We must always be ready to proclaim the Gospel of Jesus Christ before the devil and man. If we don't, something is wrong.

> . . you shall be my witnesses . . . .
>
> Acts 1:8 RSV

Lord, make us faithful in obeying Your commands. Give us the right words to say when witnessing. Above all, fill us with Your love, so others will see it.

Many people make the mistake of thinking they can measure the certainty of their salvation by their feelings. But the Word of God is the only foundation, and therefore it is essential to have a practical knowledge of the Bible.

> Open thou mine eyes, that I may behold wondrous things out of thy law.
>
> Psalms 119:18

> . . . teach me thy statutes. Make me to understand the way of thy precepts . . . I will run the way of thy commandments . . . .
>
> Psalms 119:26, 27, 32

Father, I thank You that Your Word alone gives me the certainty of my salvation. Help me to be willing to be rooted in Your Word more and more.

What is written in the Bible cannot be changed. Feelings and emotions can change. Christians are not always on the mountaintop. Act on the Word, and teach others to do so. John says, "These things have I written." Why did he write?

> . . . that you may know that you have eternal life.
>
> 1 John 5:13 RSV

Father, Your Word stands forever, and it says that we can *know* that we have eternal life. We do thank You for this assurance.

When we lose our first love, we begin to backslide, and we grow cold in our work for the Gospel. We neglect our Bible reading and prayer, and we never witness. The reason for our backsliding is always sin. Outwardly, everything may look the same, but God and we know what is wrong.

> But I have this against you, that you have abandoned the love you had at first.
>
> Revelation 2:4 RSV

Father, let Your light shine into our hearts and make us conscious of any darkness that has crept in. Bring us back to the point where we took the wrong turning. We open our hearts to You.

FEBRUARY

February 1

We must return to God, confess our sins, ask forgiveness. Then our fellowship with God will be restored and our first love will be renewed. But what if we do not feel any joy after the confession of our sins? Let us thank God for His forgiveness all the same. His promises in the Bible stand forever.

> If we confess our sins, he is faithful and just to forgive us our sins, and to cleanse us from all unrighteousness.
>
> 1 John 1:9

Thank You, Father, for this wonderful promise. Thank You that we can rely on it and that we can completely trust You. Thank You that You will restore our fellowship with You and also our joy.

February 2

A child of God has power in his struggle against Satan. However, the devil does his utmost to turn our eyes away from Jesus. He tries to get us so far away that we explain everything by our intellect.

> But the natural man receiveth not the things of the Spirit of God: for they are foolishness unto him . . . because they are spiritually discerned.
>
> 1 Corinthians 2:14

Father, You gave us Your Spirit to guide us. You will strengthen us in our struggle against Satan. Thank You for this fact.

February 3

The armor of God in Ephesians 6 is not only described as the armor of the soldiers of Jesus Christ in the victorious final battle, but also for the time of Paul, as well as for this time. Because we know that the great final battle will start soon, this armor is very important. Jesus said that these days would come, and we can see already from the newspapers that they are upon us. Let us not be afraid. These things must happen first. It is so kind of the Lord to tell us beforehand.

> . . . "Watch out that you are not deceived. For many will come in my name, claiming, 'I am he,' and 'The time is near.' Do not follow them."
>
> Luke 21:8 NIV

Lord, keep us watching and praying.

February 4

The Bible does not only give us the necessary information about Satan and demons, but also the weapons we need for this battle, so that through Jesus Christ we may be more than conquerors.

Let us keep in mind that God wants and expects us to be conquerors over the powers of darkness—not only for the sake of personal safety and for the liberation of others from the chains of slavery (though these are very important), but for His glory, so that His triumph and victory over His enemies may be demonstrated!

> And then, having drawn the sting of all the powers and authorities ranged against us, he exposed them, shattered, empty and defeated, in his own triumphant victory!
>
> Colossians 2:15 PHILLIPS

O Father, we thank You that You want to use us so that others may be made free and that it is Your will that we should be victorious, so that You may receive honor and glory.

February 5

Do you know what encouraged me lately? John 15:2. Sometimes difficulties can so depress me. Then I saw that such moments are only the back of the embroidery. On reading John 15 again and again, I began to realize that when the Lord prunes, He is very near to the branch. It caused me to feel glad, knowing the Lord was so near to me and that He pruned me that I might bring forth more fruit. I could only say, "Thank You, Lord Jesus."

> . . . every branch that does bear fruit he prunes, that it may bear more fruit.
>
> John 15:2 RSV

Yes, thank You, Lord Jesus, that You are always with me and pruning me, that I may bring forth even more fruit, that Your name may be glorified

February 6

So often I meet Christians who have the same experience as I described yesterday, and how wonderful it is then to be able to tell them of the presence of Jesus. Let us pray for one another in these times of testing, so that we cannot do anything but thank Him and not become discouraged.

When we look to Jesus, we see things, as it were, from God's side—we receive spiritual insight (*see* Colossians 1:9).

> By whom also we have access by faith . . . and rejoice in hope of the glory of God. And not only so, but we glory in tribulations also: knowing that tribulation worketh patience; And patience, experience; and experience, hope: And hope maketh not ashamed . . . .
>
> Romans 5:2–5

Father, thank You that we can always come to You in the name of Your Son, and that You will again and again fill our hearts with hope and joy. We praise and worship You.

Sometimes people say, "Why do we need Jesus to come to God?"

I once met a lady who said to me, "I have spoken with prominent people all over the world—in India, Arabia Japan, and many other countries—about the way of life in time and eternity. There were eminent persons among them, who had come to know God without Jesus Christ. You said so definitely that we need Him, but that is not true."

"You do not disagree with me, but with the Bible," I answered. "It is not I who say so." I was a bit discouraged. Sometimes I feel it is much too difficult for me to speak to learned people.

Several months later, I met this lady again, and she told me she could not forget what I had been saying. "Very, very often I had to think of your words that we need Jesus Christ to come to God."

"How great!" I answered. "You have been listening to God's voice. Go on listening, and read the Bible. There is much more He wants to say to you."

. . . no man cometh unto the Father, but by me.

John 14:6

Lord Jesus, how clearly You speak to us, so that we cannot misunderstand Your words. Help us to pass on Your words to those who do not yet know You.

February 8

Accepting Christ is not an end, but a beginning. There is a second step. We must accept Him as our Lord. When we do this, He lives His victorious life in us—He the vine, we the branches. The branch without the vine has no value at all. The vine has everlasting value. When connected with the vine, the branch can bear fruit.

> I can do all things through Christ which strengtheneth me.
>
> Philippians 4:13

Thank You, Lord, that You will give me Your strength for all the many things for which I need it. Hallelujah!

February 9

A seeking Christian will soon find out what stands in the way, if there is a hindrance. The Holy Spirit will lead him to seek forgiveness through the blood of Jesus and to accept by faith His provision for a victorious life, fully surrendered to God. Then, by faith—and only by faith—he can act upon the promises of God, and he shall receive the mighty power of God.

> Blessed are the men whose strength is in thee, in whose heart are the highways . . . . They go from strength to strength . . . .
>
> Psalms 84:5, 7 RSV

Father, You know how much I need to be filled with Your strength. You know how weak I am in myself. Thank You, that it is possible to be strong in You.

February 10

One of Satan's devices is to make us introspective. When we are looking inside ourselves, we are looking at the wrong person. We are bound to find more and more sin. We must look at Jesus. He will show us our sins in the light of His finished work upon the cross. And we shall know where we have to make restitution and get right with God and men.

> . . . let us . . . lay aside every weight, and sin which clings so closely, and let us run with perseverance the race that is set before us, looking to Jesus . . . .
>
> Hebrews 12:1, 2 RSV

Lord Jesus, we can never thank You enough that we can always rely on You. Make us willing to obey when You tell us what we should do.

February 11

My grandfather wrote to his father, "I pray that the Lord will come closer to me." But my great-grandfather wrote this answer in a letter: "A fish does not ask the water to come closer to him; a bird does not ask the air to come closer to him. The Lord is very close to us. Enjoy it."

> For in him we live, and move, and have our being . . . .
>
> Acts 17:28

Thank You, Lord, that You are near to me.

February 12

Unless you believe with all your heart, you will not see Jesus when He returns. You must invite Him to come into your heart. You must open the door. No one else can.

> Look! I have been standing at the door and I am constantly knocking. If anyone hears me calling him and opens the door, I will come in and fellowship with him and he with me.
>
> Revelation 3:20 LB

O Lord, thank You for being willing to come into my heart. Thank You for even knocking at my door. With joy I open my heart for You to enter.

February 13

A young art student was copying one of Turner's pictures in the National Gallery in London. His eyes were continually lifting from his canvas to his "master." He put nothing down that he had not just seen. He was "seeking after" Turner.

Josiah "began to seek after God" (*see* 2 Chronicles 34:3).

> . . . [He] turned to the Lord with all his heart, and with all his soul, and with all his might . . . .
>
> 2 Kings 23:25

Lord, I will seek after You—now, and this whole day during my work.

February 14

Worship has vital connections with work, just as there are nerve relationships between the heart and the hand.

We read in the stories of Ezra and Nehemiah that they first arranged the altar, then the tabernacle was rebuilt, and after that, the wall of Jerusalem.

> And they sang together .   . in praising and giving thanks unto the Lord . . . .
>
> Ezra 3:11

> Then I told them of the hand of my God which was good upon me . . . . And they said, Let us rise up and build . . . .
>
> Nehemiah 2:18

Lord, I worship You before I start my work today. I praise Your name that I belong to You with all the labor I have to do.

February 15

From the beginning of the Bible to the end, there are words of comfort and encouragement. We know that the temptation to fear is a very real one; millions of people have had it. But they have conquered, and so will you, if you take our Saviour's words of strengthening to yourself and stay yourself on them.

AMY CARMICHAEL

> Peace I leave with you, my peace I give unto you: not as the world giveth, give I unto you. Let not your heart be troubled, neither let it be afraid.
>
> John 14:27

Lord, we can never thank You enough for giving us Your peace. We praise You that we need not be troubled, need not be afraid, because of Your peace.

Jesus is the Baptizer in the Holy Spirit, and therefore the fulness of the Holy Spirit is the birthright of every child of God. But we must give room to Him, even in the corners deep down in our hearts. Then we can expect that He will do a lot in and through us.

> So, if you, for all your evil, know how to give good things to your children, how much more likely is it that your Heavenly Father will give the Holy Spirit to those who ask him!

> Luke 11:13 PHILLIPS

Lord, make us see in what respect we have not yet opened our hearts completely to Your Holy Spirit. We want to trust Him to work in us, that others may see the greatness of Your power.

February 17

Someone said, "There is no aristocracy in God's Kingdom." He was wrong. There is nothing *but* aristocracy in God's Kingdom, for we are heirs with the Son of God.

> . . . we are the children of God: And if children, then heirs . . . joint-heirs with Christ; if so be that we suffer with him, that we may be also glorified together.

> Romans 8:16, 17

Thank You, Lord, that You made us children of God and therefore heirs together with You. What a mystery that we, who are just so many specks in the vast universe, are meant to inherit the heavenly riches.

February 18

In the Bible we cannot find one single word that gives us any indication that the gifts of the Spirit were only necessary for the apostolic times. The slow "drying up" of the stream of the gifts of the Spirit is not in accordance with the biblical and historical plan of God's salvation. We must seek the reason for this in lack of faith and in the backsliding of the churches.

> . . . there are varieties of gifts, but the same Spirit   . . . But earnestly desire the higher gifts.
>
> 1 Corinthians 12:4, 31 RSV

Lord, teach each one of us the meaning of the gifts of the Spirit. Let us come with an unprejudiced heart, that You may instruct us.

February 19

If a trombone has a pure tone, the overtones vibrate, too. One does not hear them, but they give color and beauty to the tone. If, however, the tone is not pure, the overtones are silent.

If a child of God sins—if his trombone gives an impure sound— the overtones to God's glory do not resound. Because of this, a child of God feels unhappy when sinning. Then he calls out, "Father, in Jesus' name, forgive this sin," and Jesus, our Advocate, who lives and is at the right hand of the Father, says, "Father, this sin I also took upon Me." He then throws the sin into the depths of the sea, and the overtones vibrate again, giving a certain and joyful sound to our trombone.

> And you yourselves who were strangers to God, and, in fact, through the evil things you had done, his spiritual enemies, he has now reconciled through the death of Christ's body on the cross, so that he might welcome you to his presence clean and pure, without blame or reproach.
>
> Colossians 1:21 PHILLIPS

Thank You, Lord, that through Your cleansing You make our lives so harmonious.

February 20

Francis of Assisi said, "Don't you know that everyone you meet during the day should see in you something of God's love?"

Is that possible? Yes, but not by striving and trying, but rather by keeping the curtains of your heart open for the light of the Holy Spirit.

> For God, who commanded the light to shine out of darkness, hath shined in our hearts . . . .
>
> 2 Corinthians 4:6

Lord, make me a channel of Your streams of living water.

February 21

An overflowing measure of strength is at our disposal. But then, how we need it! Let us therefore live as rich as we are! This wealth is not dependent on outward circumstances. It is good to know this, because in the time of the final battle, outward circumstances are going to be very hard. You can be sure that the Lord is with us. There will always be His grace and strength. It is true that I saw my sister starve in a concentration camp, but the Lord's presence was real. He never let me down.

> . . . he is a shield for all those who take refuge in him.
>
> Psalms 18:30 RSV

Lord Jesus, in heaven we will see Your pattern of our lives, but we need to see now the most important outlines, such as Your strength being demonstrated in our weakness.

I am so glad the Bible never asks impossible things of us! How good that it does not say, "Let us look at our faith." If it did, perhaps I would say, "My faith is great." That would be pride, which is a victory of the devil. Spiritual pride ruins many blessings.

Or, which is also a victory of the devil, I might say, "Oh, that faith of mine is nothing. It does not work." We call that "defeatism."

Hudson Taylor once said, "We do not need a great faith, but faith in a great Saviour." Therefore, let us look more and more at *Jesus,* not at our faith.

> Seeing then that we have a great high priest . . Jesus the Son
> of God, let us hold fast . . . .
>
> Hebrews 4:14

Lord Jesus, we thank You that we need not look at our faith, but can look at You to receive all we need for today.

God sometimes disciplines us through illness or physical weakness. Because of my inability to travel any longer, I had to settle down. My dedication is not less, and now I experience that the message God gives me reaches more people than ever before, through the books and films I have been enabled to make in His strength in my house in California.

> . . . we know that all things work together for good to them
> that love God . . . .
>
> Romans 8:28

Thank You Lord, that You have a purpose for that suffering I have to carry. Someday I will see it; now I believe it. You never make a mistake.

February 24

If you should have one more year to live, what would you do? It may be good to think about that sometimes. Then we realize what is essential. For each one of us, it may be something different: faith to live by; peace to fill our heart; joy for others to see; wisdom to know what to give to others. Whatever it may be, it makes us more dependent on God.

> . . . my God shall supply all your need according to his riches in glory by Christ Jesus.
>
> Philippians 4:19

What a wonderful promise, Father! I can leave everything in Your hands because Your Word stands firm forever. Hallelujah!

February 25

Are you grieving over a loved one who passed away? Was he or she a child of God? Then your heart can be at peace, with the knowledge of the glory of your loved one's new home in heaven. How good it must be for that one to be at home, to be with the Lord, to see Him face-to-face!

> He will wipe away all tears from their eyes, and there shall be no more death, nor sorrow, nor crying, nor pain. All of that has gone forever.
>
> Revelation 21:4 LB

Lord, You told us You were going to prepare a place for us when You went to the Father's house. How wonderful that place will be, because there we shall see You!

February 26

I can understand your discouragement when it seems that your prayers have not been answered. But never doubt that God hears every one of your prayers, even the unusual ones. Look out for the answer, without deciding yourself what it should be like.

. . . the Father himself loves you . . . .

John 16:27 RSV

Thank You, Father, for Your love. Thank You for hearing our prayers and giving us that which You know is best for us.

February 27

A soldier must obey. He cannot serve his country if he does his own will. Jesus was obedient. He, the Creator of the world, always submitted to His Father's will. He set His face toward Jerusalem, to be crucified. He was obedient unto the death of the cross. That was His way to resurrection. It is also the way for His followers, for only the way of obedience, the way of crucifixion, leads to resurrection.

. . . bringing into captivity every thought to the obedience of Christ.

2 Corinthians 10:5

Teach us, Lord, to be obedient, as You were obedient. Show us in what way we still hold on to our own will and desires, and give us the courage to leave all in Your hands.

People have asked me, "How does God speak to you?"

Sometimes God speaks by giving me an assurance of heart, without words. It is not important *how* God answers prayers for guidance. The thing I am absolutely sure of is that God is light, not darkness. And He never leaves those who trust Him in darkness.

> This then is the message which we have heard of him, and declare unto you, that God is light, and in him is no darkness at all.
>
> 1 John 1:5

Father, we thank You that we need never walk in darkness, because You are leading us and showing us the way, step by step.

God speaks to us through His Word, the Bible; in the talks we have with Him when praying; through other people; and through that which is happening around us. If we take time to listen, we shall hear Him, and then we can go and tell others.

> . . . we have seen this day that God doth talk with man . . . .
>
> Deuteronomy 5:24

Thank You, Father, that You will always speak to us when we come to You with a heart which is willing to hear and willing to do as You say.

MARCH

March 1

God also uses our daily Bible reading to show us the way we have to take, the decision we have to make. God has promised to honor the daily use of His Word in our lives.

> I will instruct thee and teach thee in the way which thou shalt go: I will guide thee with mine eye.
>
> Psalms 32:8

Father, we know that our lives are completely in Your hands and that You are guiding us. Teach us to always trust You, even when sometimes we have to wait for Your directions as to the next step.

March 2

Another way in which God makes us know His will is by closing the doors if our decision is not the right one, or by allowing us to make a mistake, in order that we may see for ourselves that we took the wrong turn when we did not listen to Him. His Word tells us that we can hear His voice.

> And your ears shall hear a word behind you, saying, "This is the way, walk in it. . . ."
>
> Isaiah 30:21 RSV

Help us, Lord, to discern Your voice amid the many voices we hear—other people's voices and the voice of our own thoughts. Let us be near enough to hear Your soft voice.

March 3

Often God does not immediately give us a clear answer. Then we must learn to wait for Him. This waiting upon God is a blessing in itself, because we know, confidently and joyfully, that the answer will come at the time our loving Father thinks right.

> Call unto me, and I will answer thee, and shew thee great and mighty things, which thou knowest not.
>
> Jeremiah 33:3

Thank You for this promise, Father. Yes, I will call to You and wait for that which You are going to show me.

March 4

Our circumstances often are God's answers to our prayers We pray for patience, and God sends us someone demanding the utmost of our strength. We pray for selflessness, and God gives us opportunities to get rid of our self.

> . . . we also rejoice in our sufferings, because we know that suffering produces perseverance; perseverance, character; and character, hope.
>
> Romans 5:3, 4 NIV

Lord, remind us again and again that Your answers to our prayers may differ from what we think they ought to be. We wait for You to show us how to interpret Your answers.

March 5

We pray for a closer union with Jesus, and then God loosens natural relationships. Our best friends misunderstand us, or they become indifferent to us. We want to become more-faithful followers of Jesus, and then He takes us from our homeland and relations, for He said:

> So therefore, whoever of you does not renounce all that he has cannot be my disciple.
>
> Luke 14:33 RSV

Lord, we pray, make us willing to let go of everything and count it but loss, because we do want to follow You.

March 6

We pray for peace, and suddenly everything in us and around us is in a turmoil, in order that we should learn to rely on God and trust Him completely.

> When he giveth quietness, who then can make trouble? . . .
>
> Job 34:29

Thank You, Lord, that You are able to give quietness into our hearts, when there is nothing but unrest around us and even in us. Thank You that You are Victor over it all.

March 7

We pray for victory, and the things of this world pull us into a whirlpool of temptation.

> . . . this is the victory that overcomes the world, our faith.
>
> 1 John 5:4 RSV

Lord, evermore give us this victory.

March 8

We need men and women who are full of the Holy Spirit, in whom the gifts of grace are active. Such people can show the world that God is alive.

> But grace was given to each of us according to the measure of Christ's gift.
>
> Ephesians 4:7 RSV

Lord, we want to be one of those who can show the world that You are alive today. Thank You for the grace given to each one of us, grace which is never ending.

March 9

We must measure the value of the gifts in accordance with what is written in Holy Scripture, where they are shown to be important. When the Bible says, "desire spiritual gifts" (1 Corinthians 14:1), we cannot change this into "keep away from the gifts of the Spirit." We can fight against their misuse, but never against the gifts themselves.

What a responsibility! God offers to His Church these gifts, but on the condition that we pray for them. Very often we do not do that, and therefore we are so poor and in want.

> There are different kinds of gifts . . . All these are the work of
> one and the same Spirit, and he gives them to each man, just as
> he determines.
>
> 1 Corinthians 12:4, 11 NIV

Thank You, Father, that each one of us has received gifts. Open
our eyes to them, that we may use them to glorify You.

March 10

Follow the pathway of obedience. Let the Word of God do its
own work in you, and you will be used by God far beyond your
own powers.

F. B. Meyer said, "God does not fill with His Holy Spirit those
who believe in the fulness of the Spirit, or those who desire Him,
but those who obey Him."

> Seeing ye have purified your souls in obeying the truth through
> the Spirit unto unfeigned love of the brethren, see that ye love
> one another . . . .
>
> 1 Peter 1:22

Father, help me to be always obedient to what Your Word tells me,
so that You can use me.

March 11

No one can trust God who does not obey Him. Obedience is the
root of trust. In Jesus' life, trusting went quite without saying,
because, for Him, obedience went without saying.

> . . . Hath the Lord as great delight in burnt offerings and
> sacrifices, as in obeying the voice of the Lord? . . .
>
> 1 Samuel 15:22

Teach us, Father, always to be willing to listen to Your voice and to
be obedient, that we may bring joy to Your heart.

March 12

Although God's love never changes, we do not always live in the joy of it. When sin comes between God and our soul, as a dark cloud between the sun and the earth, our communion with Him is broken. Let us therefore avoid everything that might rob us of enjoying God's immeasurable love.

> . . it was by the generosity of God, the free giving of the grace of the one man Jesus Christ, that the love of God overflowed for the benefit of all men.
>
> Romans 5:15 PHILLIPS

Help us, Lord, to put aside everything that hinders our enjoying Your love, everything that breaks our communion with You, because we cannot live without it.

March 13

Some Christians live in bondage. The reason they are not free may lie in the past. It may be a sin; it may be because they do not forgive. It may be a tie with the wrong person, or even a tie with the right person, one who really follows the Lord.

> If the Son therefore shall make you free, ye shall be free indeed.
>
> John 8:36

Lord, show me what still ties me down. Open my eyes, that I may see and ask You to cleanse me.

Our sins can be shown to us in two very different ways.

In the first place, Satan accuses the saints day and night. Again and again he tell us our sins, until we become quite desperate. He says, "Now you can see how you really are. That which you have done is completely according to your character, and that will never change."

If, however, the Holy Spirit shows us our sins, He does it in the full light of the finished work at the cross. He says to us, "For this sin Jesus died. He bore the punishment."

He is alive, and it is His will that you become more than conqueror. Repent and turn away from your sin in His strength. His blood cleanses. He gives us the victory. He sends the answer, and the Holy Spirit enables us to close our ears to the accuser.

> And they overcame him by the blood of the Lamb, and by the word of their testimony . . . .
>
> Revelation 12:11

Thank You, Lord, for the power of Your blood. Thank You for giving Your life for us. Thank You that You are Victor forever.

I have met many young people who were set free because they wrote to their parents: "Will you, please, forgive me what I did wrong? I want to forgive you the things that you did not do right."

They became a blessing to their parents. After having written a letter like the above, some of them could bring their parents to the Lord.

> Admit your faults to one another and pray for each other so that you may be healed . . . .
>
> James 5:16 LB

Father, help us to forgive, as You have forgiven us.

March 16

How the enemy uses human channels! You can only be made free from that when you break off certain friendships in the power of Jesus Christ.

We are not ready for His coming, if all is not well between God and us and between other people and us.

> Follow peace with all men, and holiness, without which no man shall see the Lord.
>
> Hebrews 12:14

Show me, Lord, the things I must put right with others, the things that are hindering me from being an open channel. Make me ready for Your coming.

March 17

It can also be that we must be made free from a tie with the right person: someone who really follows the Lord. This I had to learn myself. A vision my sister Betsie had in the concentration camp where she died showed me the work that I would have to do after the war. When the time had come that I had to let go of this work, I felt very unhappy and depressed.

Then a sister in the Lord showed me that also a tie with a beloved one who has died can be wrong. In the name of Jesus I was made free from it, and the Lord gave me deep peace.

> It is better to trust in the Lord than to put confidence in man.
>
> Psalms 118:8

> The Lord openeth the eyes of the blind . . . .
>
> Psalms 146:8

Thank You, Father, that You open our eyes, that we may see clearly whether we really trust You more than a human being, however dear to us.

March 18

Not all prisoners are behind bars. There are prisoners of self, lust, money, ambition, or pride. You can be liberated today. Confess and be cleansed, and in Jesus' power you can turn away 100 percent.

Who hath delivered us from the power of darkness . . . .

Colossians 1:13

Search me, God, and show me if I am a prisoner. Show me the cross where all was finished, so that I may understand that it made me free.

March 19

Are you a prisoner of lust?

You thought it would make you happy, but you know now that such bondage is hard and unhappy. There is an answer: It is Jesus. He carried this sin at the cross, and He lives, and He is willing to liberate you this very moment. Turn away; come to Him. He hates your sin. He loves you.

. . . I did not come to judge the world but to save the world.

John 12:47 RSV

Lord, in Your strength; I turn away and come to You.

March 20

Are you in the prison of self?

. . . Anyone who wants to follow me must put aside his own desires and conveniences and carry his cross with him every day and *keep close to me!*

Luke 9:23 LB

Lord, I thought it meant losing my life when I surrendered to You, but I see that it is the opposite. It is gaining my life to give myself to You.

March 21

Are you in the prison of occultism? You did it just for fun when you went to that fortune-teller, when you let him look at your palm, when he told you what was going to happen and it really did happen. But now you are in darkness. You came, because of that "fun," into the territory of the demons, and they are tough. But there is One who is stronger.

Tell it to Jesus. Repent, and He will set you free.

> So use every piece of God's armor to resist the enemy . . . when it is all over, you will still be standing up.
>
> Ephesians 6:13 LB

Forgive me, Lord Jesus, and liberate me. I praise You for Your cleansing blood.

March 22

Are you in the bondage of smoking, alcohol, or drugs? Realize that you are in a spiritual battle. We do not have to fight against flesh and blood, but against the very representatives of the headquarters of evil. But they are conquered enemies.

When I stood in front of death in the concentration camp, I saw things so realistically and simply. There was I; there was the devil. He is much stronger than I. But there was Jesus. He is much, very much stronger than the devil, and with Him, I am stronger than the devil.

> Be strong and of good courage, do not fear or be in dread of them: for it is the Lord your God who goes with you; he will not fail you or forsake you.
>
> Deuteronomy 31:6 RSV

Thank You, Lord Jesus for the perfect logistics of Your armor.

March 23

The Lord opens doors and sets the captives free; not only those behind iron doors, but also captives of sin, selfishness, and other bonds. Are you free indeed? If not, Jesus can make you free. Put your weak hand in His strong hand. He said:

> Come unto me, all ye that labour and are heavy laden, and I will give you rest.

> Matthew 11:28

Lord, You know how tired and burdened I sometimes am. I come to You today, just as I am. Give me Your rest.

March 24

A compromise is fatal. The devil, who is a liar, tells you that a little bit of "yes, but . . . " is so much easier than "yes, Jesus." That is a lie! Every day with Jesus is better than the day before, but He is not willing for you to be only a member of a spiritual insurance company. He is our Saviour. He has bought you with His blood—a very high price. He is the King of kings, the Son of God.

> Stay always within the boundaries where God's love can reach and bless you . . . .

> Jude 21 LB

Lord, I surrender all. Set my feet on victory ground.

March 25

Are you a backslider? The enemy tells you that now you cannot go on with the Lord. But read what Jesus told about the good shepherd in Luke 15:3–7. He left the ninety-nine good sheep at home and went to seek the one naughty, stupid sheep. After he found it, he rejoiced.

The Lord Jesus will rejoice when you come again to Him. This moment, He is telling you, "Come to me, you who are heavy laden, and I will give you rest" (Matthew 11:28).

> . . . there will be . . . joy in heaven over one sinner who repents . . . .
>
> Luke 15:7 RSV

Lord Jesus, I am a lost sheep. Thank You for seeking me, that I may come back to You.

March 26

An unrepented sin is a continued sin. Don't be careless about it. You do not need two different poisons to be killed. If you do not repent, the blood of Christ cannot cleanse you, and you cannot receive eternal life.

> . . . every man shall die for his own sin.
>
> 2 Chronicles 25:4

O Lord, help me to bring every sin which you show me to You at once, asking forgiveness. Let me never forget what even the smallest sin cost You.

March 27

As He cleanses our lives, so He fills them to overflowing with the Holy Spirit. Everything that the light of God shows up as sin, we can confess and carry to the fountain of the water of life, and it is gone from God's sight and from our hearts.

> . . . What God has cleansed, you must not call common.
>
> Acts 10:15 RSV

Lord, keep us from the sin of remembered sins. That sin we have confessed is gone forever. Hallelujah!

March 28

Did you conquer? Not yet? Does that mean defeat? You are not the first one to experience that. Jesus sometimes seems to lose a battle, but He never loses a war. Soak in the Word of God. The Bible shows that there is much to fight, but Jesus is Victor.

> "And they will fight against you, but they will not overcome you, for I am with you to deliver you," declares the Lord.
>
> Jeremiah 1:19 NAS

Lord Jesus, it all seems defeat, but I know in my heart that You are Victor. Make me more than conqueror.

March 29

How wonderful it is, that Jesus Christ came into this world to save sinners! On Calvary we see the awful sinfulness of sin. But we also see Him, who came to destroy sin.

> . . . For this purpose the Son of God was manifested, that he might destroy the works of the devil.
>
> 1 John 3:8

Lord Jesus, how can we ever thank You enough, that You were willing to come into this world to save us and that You came to destroy the works of the devil? We thank You that You are the Victor!

March 30

In the Bible we find a wonderful prayer of worship by David. Do you join David in his prayer? Do you belong to those who praise and honor Him? If not, will you not turn to Him today?

> Thine, O Lord, is the greatness, and the power, and the glory, and the victory, and the majesty: for all that is in the heaven and in the earth is thine; thine is the kingdom, O Lord, and thou art exalted as head above all.
>
> 1 Chronicles 29:11

Lord God, we come to You with thanksgiving, and we praise You for Your exceeding greatness. If there is anyone among us who is not yet able to join us, we pray You will work in his heart, that he may come to You, accepting You as his Lord and Saviour.

March 31

Time must be set apart for prayer. Prayer is the key for the day, the lock for the night.

> Be always on the watch, and pray . . . .
>
> Luke 21:36 NIV

Make us ever more conscious of the fact that prayer is essential for our life with You, Lord. Only then shall we be able to hear Your voice.

APRIL

April 1

Praying means listening to God's directions and instructions with a heart that is open toward Him; it is a talk between a Father and His child. Having an open heart means being willing to do whatever He says.

> . . . Speak, Lord; for thy servant heareth . . . .
>
> 1 Samuel 3:9

Yes, Lord, we also pray: Speak, for we want to hear. Even though so often we do not listen and are not willing, yet You know that we long to hear You speak. Make us obedient to Your voice.

April 2

Lack of intercession is sin. Did you promise to pray for someone in need, someone who is ill, or a missionary? Did you keep that promise? If not, do you realize this to be a sin? Go to the Lord with it and ask Him to forgive you.

> . . . God forbid that I should sin against the Lord in ceasing to pray for you . . . .
>
> 1 Samuel 12:23

Lord, make me faithful in praying for others, and keep me faithful.

54

April 3

One day in Germany, a woman came to me. Her face was distorted by hatred. She was full of her own virtues and other people's faults. I just let her talk and listened. Suddenly it was as if something in her broke down, and she confessed that she had an empty heart.

I told her, "I know One who can fill the emptiness of your heart, but you can only come to Him with a prayer for mercy, and that you will not be able to do."

She called out, "I am a hypocrite. I see it now. Is there no mercy for me?"

I pointed out to her the great simple love of Jesus for sinners, and though she was not completely free, her attitude was much more humble when she left. Afterwards, I learned that a man in the adjoining room had been praying during our conversation. How wonderful intercession is!

> I exhort therefore, that, first of all, supplications, prayers, intercessions, and giving of thanks, be made for all men.

> 1 Timothy 2:1

Thank You, Father, that we can all take part in praying and interceding for others. Thank You that You always hear us and that You will do more than we can ever think of. We praise You!

April 4

How important are our prayers in God's eyes?

Do you know that not one of your prayers is lost? Your prayers—for your son, your daughter, your mother, your father, your friend, or whoever you prayed for—are so costly in God's eyes that they are stored in heaven.

> And another angel came and stood at the altar, having a golden censer; and there was given unto him much incense, that he should offer it with the prayers of all saints upon the golden altar which was before the throne.
>
> Revelation 8:3

Lord, forgive me that I have underestimated my intercessions. I prayed to You in Jesus' name, and therefore they are so precious. Hallelujah!

April 5

Each one of us can pray for the leaders of the countries, just as we can pray for the salvation of unbelievers, for strength and encouragement for those in need—in fact for everyone. The Bible tells us over and over again that this is what we should do.

> And the Lord turned the captivity of Job, when he prayed for his friends . . . .
>
> Job 42:10

Father, how wonderful it is that You allow us to come to You with all that occupies our minds, but also with other people's needs. Thank You that we can unburden ourselves and leave everything with You. Thank You for hearing us.

April 6

In our days there is much talk about peace between the nations. Everybody knows how greatly this is needed. Many think that talking about peace will help. But if it is not from God, and the leaders do not receive wisdom from above, it will not be of much avail.

> The way of peace they know not; and there is no judgment in their goings: they have made them crooked paths: whosoever goeth therein shall not know peace.
>
> Isaiah 59:8

Lord, teach us the way of peace. Keep us from going along crooked paths. We only want to follow You.

April 7

Often words of peace sound so beautiful, but they are only a façade. There is no real peace behind the words. If, however, we choose for peace through Jesus Christ, the real beauty will be there. God will humble our hearts, and then we shall be able to go the path of real peace.

> . . . there shall be an highway for the remnant of his people . . . .
>
> Isaiah 11:16

Thank You, Father, that through Jesus Christ You cleared the path of peace for us and that He promised to give us His peace.

When the Church and its believers think of peace, they must always keep in mind that they are on God's side. God always brings light into darkness. Without power from above, we cannot discern. We must pray for the church leaders to be filled with the Holy Spirit.

> First of all, then, I urge that supplications, prayers, intercessions, and thanksgivings be made for . . . kings and all who are in high positions, that we may lead a quiet and peaceable life . . . .
>
> 1 Timothy 2:1, 2 RSV

Make us more faithful, Lord, in praying for those who have the great responsibility of leading the nations. Give them Your wisdom for all the decisions they have to make.

We live in the pause before the last trumpet sound. This is the great advent for the whole world. Jesus is coming, and will make all things new.

> . . . Behold, I make all things new . . . .
>
> Revelation 21:5

Lord, I look forward to Your coming. Give me inspiration about how to use my time.

April 10

There is a great battle going on in the invisible world. The enemy will try with all his might to alienate us from God, to destroy our faith in Jesus Christ, and to make us rebellious against God. We can shut our eyes to the danger and not see where the course of world history will lead us. But Jesus says:

> Watch ye therefore, and pray always, that ye may be accounted worthy to escape all these things that shall come to pass, and to stand before the Son of man.
>
> Luke 21:36

Lord, You alone are able to keep us, that we may be able to stand before You. Give us the strength and keep us from falling away from You.

April 11

Once when I was in the hospital, I learned something. I was in much pain, and I remembered the pain Jesus suffered for me, for my sins, and for the sins of the whole world. I remembered His love for the world, His love for me, and I received new strength.

I also remembered that He went the way to glory through suffering. Isn't that also guidance? If we follow Him in suffering, He will also lead us to glory.

> . . . we are the children of God: And if children, then heirs; heirs of God, and joint-heirs with Christ; if so be that we suffer with him, that we may be also glorified together.
>
> Romans 8:16, 17

Guide me continuously, Father. And if suffering is part of the way, remind me that this too is meant to bring glory to You. Thank You that You are my Helper.

Are you a child of God? God is waiting for you to come to Him and tell Him you want to be His child, if you do not yet belong to Him. Everything that was needed to make you God's child was finished many centuries ago on Calvary, when Jesus died for you.

Today He is asking you—and I may ask you in His name—"Do you want to become a child of God?" If you say, "Yes, Lord, I want to, because I love You," He will say, "For a long time I have been waiting for that answer. It is good—now you are My child."

> . . . as many as received him, to them gave he power to become the sons of God, even to them that believe on his name.
>
> John 1:12

Lord, we thank You that we may know You as our Lord and Saviour. We pray for those who have not yet received You. Open their eyes, that they may see.

Jesus' cross seemed the end of love, but it was the great result of love and the beginning of salvation for all who come to Him, because they will always be with Him.

> The Lord thy God in the midst of thee is mighty; he will save, he will rejoice over thee with joy; he will rest in his love, he will joy over thee with singing.
>
> Zephaniah 3:17

Father, keep us close to You, fill us with Your love, so that indeed You may rejoice over us.

When God calls you, don't look over your shoulder to see who is following you. *You* have to answer Him. Most likely, God will call somebody else for another task. And so you and I each work in His service, in the place He appoints for us.

> And he gave some, apostles; and some, prophets; and some, evangelists; and some, pastors and teachers; For the perfecting of the saints, for the work of the ministry, for the edifying of the body of Christ.
>
> Ephesians 4:11, 12

Thank You, Father, that when You call us, You also show us where You want us to serve You, fitting us into the whole, that Your name may be glorified.

I cannot know the full impact of sin until I see it in the light of Calvary. I see the awfulness of sin, be it expressed in small sins or in big ones, when I realize what even the smallest sin cost God: He gave His only Son to die on the cross.

> He that spared not his own Son, but delivered him up for us all . . . .
>
> Romans 8:32

Father, I can never thank You enough for Your love for us—even for me. Take my life into Your hands and let it be to Your glory.

April 16

What does the cross show us? What do we see when our eyes are opened? We see that our sins are laid on Jesus, and that His righteousness is placed on us.

Jesus had legions of angels available, which could have been an overwhelming defense. Nobody could have done Him any harm without His allowing it, but He did not use His defense. Through His obedience, He made His defense available to us—to you and to me.

> . . . he humbled himself, and became obedient unto death, even the death of the cross.
>
> Philippians 2:8

> that you may be blameless and innocent, children of God without blemish in the midst of a crooked and perverse generation . . . .
>
> Philippians 2:15 RSV

Thank You, Lord, for what You did for me. Show me what I can do for You.

April 17

We must have assurance of salvation. There can be nothing vague or uncertain in our relationship with Jesus Christ and with God.

> These things have I written unto you that believe on the name of the Son of God; that ye may know that ye have eternal life . . . .
>
> 1 John 5:13

Father, thank You that I *know* that I have eternal life, because Your Son told us that everyone who believes that He is Lord *has* this life.

62

April 18

Don't try to escape the cross.

> Whoever does not bear his own cross and come after me,
> cannot be my disciple.

Luke 14:27 RSV

Lord, make me willing to follow You every new day.

April 19

The blood of Jesus Christ has great power! There is perhaps not a phrase in the Bible that is so full of secret truths as "the blood of Jesus." It is the secret of His Incarnation, when Jesus took our flesh and blood; the secret of His obedience unto death, when He gave His life at the Cross of Calvary; the secret of His love that went beyond all understanding when He bought us with His blood; the secret of the enemy and the secret of our eternal salvation.

> he entered once for all into the Holy Place, taking . . . his own
> blood, thus securing an eternal redemption.

Hebrews 9:12 RSV

Help us, Lord, that we may more fully understand the value of Your blood. It is hidden from our natural minds, but please reveal it to our spirits.

April 20

Why does the devil hate it when the blood of Christ is spoken of? Because it reminds him of his defeat on Calvary through the death of Jesus, who gave His blood for us. But it also reminds him of Jesus' life, of the Risen One, to whom we may always go with our sins. That is why the devil is afraid of it. The blood of Jesus Christ has great power.

> And they have conquered him by the blood of the Lamb and by the word of their testimony, for they loved not their lives even unto death.
>
> Revelation 12:11 RSV

Father, we thank You that we can conquer the devil through the blood of Your Son and by our testimony. Keep us steadfast in the faith and help us to give a clear testimony to those who do not know You yet.

April 21

Are you prepared for the coming of Jesus? Am I prepared for the coming of Jesus? It is wonderful that the Bible clearly says that only by full surrender are we made ready for His coming again. If it depended on us, then one day we would be successful, but the next day it would be just the opposite.

> . . . Jesus Christ: Who shall also confirm you unto the end, that ye may be blameless in the day of our Lord Jesus Christ
>
> 1 Corinthians 1:7, 8

Thank You, Lord, that You are our strength and that, if only we surrender to Your will, You will keep us to the end.

April 22

There is still a tremendous struggle in sight, but the moment is coming when our sanctification will be complete. Yes, the best is yet to be! One day there will be an end to the battle. Then there will be complete victory: the victory through Jesus Christ!

> May the God of peace make you holy through and through. May you be kept sound in spirit, mind and body, blameless until the coming of our Lord Jesus Christ.
>
> 1 Thessalonians 5:23 PHILLIPS

How we long to be made holy through and through, Lord. Make us willing to let Your Spirit work in us.

April 23

When the marching orders of our King are given, and they seem very exacting, we need not fear. He Himself gives us the courage, the faithfulness, and the strength to obey Him. "Go in this thy might," He says when He has given us, through the Holy Spirit, the fruit of the Spirit: faithfulness and strength.

> . . . if we are faithless he always remains faithful. He cannot deny his own nature.
>
> 2 Timothy 2:13 PHILLIPS

Thank You, Lord, that we never need go in our own strength. Thank You that You Yourself provide all we lack. Only, help us to be faithful.

April 24

It is essential that we realize in these days that Jesus is *the* Conqueror! To stand at His side, to follow Him, to be hidden with Him in God—that is the safe position for every soldier of Jesus in this time and in the coming final battle.

> Do not conform yourselves to the standards of this world, but let God transform you inwardly by a complete change of your mind. Then you will be able to know the will of God—what is good and is pleasing to him and is perfect.

> Romans 12:2 TEV

Lord, we thank You that You will never leave us alone. If only we abide in You, we shall remain hidden with You in God, and we shall be able to overcome.

April 25

Are you afraid to witness? How do you make the choice as to whom and where to witness? Remember, your mailman also has an eternity to win or to lose.

> Go ye therefore, and teach all nations . . . .

> Matthew 28:19

Lord, show me to whom I must tell the joyful news of the Gospel. I will obey Your choice, not mine.

April 26

Either we have let go of "self" or we have not. The proof is in our reactions to that which happens to us. Many people are correct in their actions, but not in their reactions. Those around us are watching for our reactions. Do we realize that these may cause others to turn to Jesus or to turn away from Him?

Look carefully then how you walk . . . .

Ephesians 5:15 RSV

Thank You, Lord, for Your grace, given to work in us, that others may see You and turn to You.

April 27

If people don't see Jesus in the Bible, this is not your fault. But if they don't see Him in your life, that is your fault.

he who says he abides in him ought to walk in the same way in which he walked.

1 John 2:6 RSV

Help me, Lord, as I live through each day, to really abide in You, that others may see You and come to You as their Lord and Saviour.

April 28

Nobody will know what you mean when you say that God is love, if you do not live that love. God Himself will provide the opportunities for doing so.

> . . . as I have loved you, that ye also love one another. By this shall all men know that ye are my disciples, if ye have love one to another.
>
> John 13:34, 35

Lord, evermore give us this love.

April 29

Once I spoke to a group of students. I realized that the leaders did not quite know what to do with me—such an *old* woman! Was *she* to speak to the students? Nevertheless, they gave me an opportunity to give a testimony.

A few years ago, I heard what happened after that. One of the leaders came to me and said, "Do you remember what the Lord did through you during that week? For many students, the week was decisive for their lives."

Whenever I hear such a thing, I am reminded of heaven. What will it be like, when others come to us and say, "You invited me. Here I am!"? Yes, there you will see how the Lord blessed your testimony, the comforting word you passed on here on earth. God's Word never returns empty. Hallelujah!

> . . . Blessed are all they that put their trust in him.
>
> Psalms 2:12

Thank You, Father, that You are willing to use even me, and that I may pass on to others what You gave me.

Beware of criticism of your fellow Christians. In Romans 14, we are told not to criticize any of God's servants. The Holy Spirit gives us the wisdom we need to know what is discernment and what is wrong criticism.

> Why, then, do you criticise your brother's actions, why do you try to make him look small? We shall all be judged one day, not by each other's standards or even by our own, but by the judgment of God.
>
> Romans 14:10 PHILLIPS

Lord, forgive my criticism. Give me the fruit of the Holy Spirit—love—then I will have helpful discernment.

MAY

May 1

Discernment is God's call to intercession, never to faultfinding.

> Forbearing one another, and forgiving one another, if any man
> have a quarrel against any . . . .
>
> Colossians 3:13

O Lord, today let me see people as it were with Your eyes.

May 2

It is a spiritual law that a man only gets peace when he himself is
willing to forgive without reserve.

> . . . forgive our sins—for we have forgiven those who sinned
> against us . . . .
>
> Luke 11:4 LB

Thank You, Lord, that You brought into my heart God's love
through the Holy Spirit. Thank You, Father, that Your love in me is
stronger than my unforgiveness, my resentment—yes—my hatred.
Hallelujah!

May 3

The best indication of how strong you are is whether you can love your enemies. God knows you cannot do it yourself. You need His love in your heart. He will do it.

> And those who belong to Christ Jesus have crucified the flesh with its passions and desires.
>
> Galatians 5:24 RSV

Lord Jesus, so often we have not shown You to others because we were too much taken up with ourselves. So often we did not let Your love work in us, forgetting that those around us were watching to see how we would react to our enemies. Forgive us and cleanse us.

May 4

God sometimes keeps us waiting for an answer to our prayers, but He never keeps us waiting one single second for an answer to our prayer for forgiveness. He hates sin, and is only too glad to sweep it away. He loves the sinner, and is only too happy to receive him. And He is able because Jesus bore the punishment for our sins at the cross. The Father loves the Son and delights to work out His image and likeness in us.

> . . . . "Let every one who names the name of the Lord depart from iniquity."
>
> 2 Timothy 2:19 RSV

Father, we know You hear every prayer of ours. And yet at times we think You are not hearing and we become impatient. Forgive us for doubting Your love, as this is also sin. We want to obey Your commandment to depart from iniquity.

May 5

"Be filled with the Spirit" is the most joyful commandment of the Bible. It is the Holy Spirit who gives us the fruit and the gifts we need in the world to be the light, to be the bread, to be the salt of the earth, and who gives us eyes to see.

> that the God of our Lord Jesus Christ, the Father of glory, may give you a spirit of wisdom and of revelation in the knowledge of him, having the eyes of your hearts enlightened, that you may know what is the hope to which he has called you, what are the riches of his glorious inheritance in the saints.

> Ephesians 1:17, 18 RSV

Lord, here is my life. Take me, fill me, use me.

May 6

Dr. F. B. Meyer has told how his early Christian life was marred and his ministry paralyzed, just because he kept back one key of the bunch of keys he had given to the Lord. Every key, save one.

The key of one room was kept for personal use, the Lord was shut out, and the effects of the incomplete consecration were found in a lack of power, a lack of assurance, a lack of joy and peace.

> He that loveth . . . more than me is not worthy of me . . . .

> Matthew 10:37

Forgive me my compromise. Take me 100 percent, Lord.

May 7

Most people seem to settle for mere animal-life necessities: enough to eat, a comfortable place to sleep, and companionship with a similar being. These three elements satisfy dogs. Yet surely, each human being, having another dimension—a God-conscious spirit—demands more than a lower creature. What is your highest ambition? What purpose or objective do you have? Are you really alive, or just existing? Jesus gives a clear answer about life:

. . . I came that they may have life, and have it abundantly.

John 10:10 RSV

Forgive me, Father, that I was too quickly content with a shallow life, when You had offered a joy unspeakable and full of glory through Jesus Christ.

May 8

Surrender includes letting the wrong things go out of our lives. The things we know are wrong, or that we are doubtful about, must be completely abandoned.

. . . sin no more . . . .

John 5:14

Help us, Lord, to make a clean cut with everything we know is wrong. Thank You, that Your Spirit in us causes us to feel uneasy about all we have to put away.

The Lord knew all about Nathanael. He told him: "When you were under the fig tree in that secret meditation, when your wishes and desires were being born, I saw you." Nathanael saw a side of Jesus that was most encouraging. He suddenly knew: He knows, He loves, He cares. It was the joyful beginning of his discipleship.

Do you know who Jesus is? Do you realize that He sees you, He loves you? Do become His disciple.

> . . . Follow me.

> John 1:43

O Lord, what a joy that I may do it. Yes, Lord, yes. Come into my life, my heart. Fill me with Your Holy Spirit.

The way to be ready is by surrendering to Him who longs for us and who is willing to prepare us for His return. Paul wrote to the Thessalonians:

> And the Lord make you to increase and abound in love one toward another, and toward all men . . . .

> 1 Thessalonians 3:12

Yes, Lord, we want to surrender more fully to You. Make us willing for You to prepare us for Your return, so that we may be found ready on that wonderful day.

May 11

Surrender! The potter cannot form the vessel, if all of the clay needed is not put into his hands, or if we are not willing to leave it there—every bit of it.

> Woe unto him that striveth with his Maker! Let the potsherd strive with the potsherds of the earth. Shall the clay say to him that fashioneth it, What makest thou? . . .
>
> Isaiah 45:9

> But now, O Lord, thou art our father; we are the clay, and thou our potter . . . .
>
> Isaiah 64:8

Our Father, we pray You anew, form us and make us vessels to Your honor. Keep us from struggling against You. We thank You that we can leave it all to You—our Potter *and* our Father!

May 12

It is very difficult for us to accept illness. Once, when I was a young woman, I had a long illness. It took many days before I could surrender and accept the situation.

I learned to thank God, but I could not understand why He wanted me to lie in bed, imprisoned by the walls of my little room. Every day I prayed for peace in my heart, and finally the moment came when I could say, "Yes, Lord, You know best."

> We pray that you will be strengthened from God's glorious power, so that you may be able to pass through any experience and endure it with joy. You will be able to thank the Father because you are privileged to share the lot of the saints who are living in the light.
>
> Colossians 1:11, 12 PHILLIPS

Father, I thank You that You always enable me to pass through any experience You think fit for me. Teach me more and more to accept everything as coming from You. Thank You that You never make a mistake in any yielded life.

May 13

Is every illness out of the plan of God? I should not say so, for after all, we are training for higher service, and I know that suffering can be part of that training.

However, giving too much attention to little symptoms is playing into the hands of the enemy. He uses illness to depress us, until we see things out of all proportion to their real value. So we must also turn to the Lord with those "little" symptoms. He knows how difficult it can be to work when feeling unwell, and He is able to give the strength needed for that which we must do. Perhaps He is just saying to us that we should draw apart for a little while and let ourselves be refreshed by Himself.

> You can throw the whole weight of your anxieties upon him,
> for you are his personal concern.
>
> 1 Peter 5:7 PHILLIPS

Thank You, Lord, that You are my Helper, that You are taking care of me in whatever circumstances I may be, and that I can always trust in You and rest in You.

May 14

In God's faithfulness lies eternal security. I once asked my father what predestination was. He answered, "The ground on which I build my faith is not in me, but in the faithfulness of God."

> . . . God's firm foundation stands, bearing this seal: "The Lord knows those who are his," and, "Let every one who names the name of the Lord depart from iniquity."
>
> 2 Timothy 2:19 RSV

Father, thank You for Your Word, which tells us over and over again that You know each one of us who is Your child and that You also know all our needs.

May 15

Suffering is God's thorny but blessed road to wonderful victory. We must learn to remain faithful.

> Do not fear what you are about to suffer . . . Be faithful unto death, and I will give you the crown of life.
>
> Revelation 2:10 RSV

Lord, You know how often I fear when hearing of suffering and when suffering myself. Thank You for Your promises. Thank You for Your victory. Make me victorious.

May 16

There are things that are not essentially wrong for others, yet are a hindrance to ourselves. We can know this in different ways: we are uneasy about them; we argue about them with our conscience; we ask other people's advice, hoping they will tell us what we would like to hear.

Let us heed these warnings. Such things must be laid aside in the strength which Jesus waits to give. Let us ask Him to deal with them for us.

> Since we have these promises, beloved, let us cleanse ourselves from every defilement . . . and make holiness perfect in the fear of God.
>
> 2 Corinthians 7:1 RSV

And, Lord, we thank You that we do not need to do this in our own strength, but that You will give us Your strength and make us victorious.

May 17

It is very easy to look only at the outside of a person, but we must remember that God looks on the inside, and so should we. Often the person who least looks like it has a deep yearning inside to know more of our Lord.

> Search me, O God, and know my heart: try me, and know my thoughts: And see if there be any wicked way in me, and lead me in the way everlasting.
>
> Psalms 139:23, 24

Father, forgive me for so often judging others from what is seen on the outside. Give me more of Your love, that I may see them as You do.

May 18

Our critics are the unpaid guardians of our soul. If what they say is true, then do something about it. If it is not true, just put it aside and don't let it influence you.

> Be gentle and ready to forgive; never hold grudges . . . .
>
> Colossians 3:13 LB

Thank You, Lord, for those who give me loving criticism. Let it draw me closer to You.

May 19

We all need the Holy Spirit to enlarge our hearts, so they may contain more of the "joy unspeakable and full of glory"—God's abundant love *in* us.

> . . . everlasting joy shall be unto them.

> Isaiah 61:7

Our Father, we pray that Your Holy Spirit may work in us, so that our hearts may contain more of this abundant joy. We do rejoice in Your love, and can never thank You enough for it. Help us to show it to others.

May 20

Worry is a cycle of inefficient thoughts whirling around a center of fear. But God does not want His children to be fearful, and the best way to overcome fear is through the Word of God.

> Let not your heart be troubled . . . .

> John 14:1

> . . . I will trust, and not be afraid . . . .

> Isaiah 12:2

Yes, Lord, I will trust. Thank You for telling me I need not worry.

May 21

There are times when we worry about everything, even about our salvation. It is the devil who tries to pull us away from God. As soon as we look up at the cross, however, we see again that it is "not I, but Christ." God sees us in Christ. He can fulfill the law, and He did it when He died on the cross. Our salvation lies in Him, so we need never doubt.

> . . . our Lord Jesus Christ, who died for us so that . . . we might live with him.
>
> 1 Thessalonians 5:9, 10 RSV

We thank You, Lord, that You died for each one of us, in order that we might live. Thank You that this is forever true.

May 22

We can have the fruit of the Spirit. One sign of the fruit is peace, and we can know that He will keep those in perfect peace whose trust is in Him.

Someone said that there are millions of depressed people in America. Are they all unbelievers, or are there also Christians among them? If that is so, it means that they do not know their defense. You can pray for the many depressed Christians: "Open their eyes, that they may see that their tomorrow is in God's hand." It is the Holy Spirit who turns our eyes in the right direction.

> For God hath not given us the spirit of fear; but of power, and of love, and of a sound mind.
>
> 2 Timothy 1:7

Lord, what a joy that there is an answer for everyone. You, Lord Jesus, are the answer.

You have an Advocate with the Father—Jesus. He takes your sins on His own shoulders and cleanses you with His blood. When He died on the cross, He identified Himself with your death, and now you and I must identify ourselves with His life.

If you confess a sin as soon as you are conscious of it, you can say:

> For our sake he made him to be sin who knew no sin, so that in him we might become the righteousness of God.

> 2 Corinthians 5:21 RSV

Father, cause us to realize more and more what it means that Your Son Jesus Christ was made to be sin—for us.

It is the fan of the air-conditioner that causes the cold air to be distributed all over the house. The Spirit penetrates our whole being in the same way, giving light and life and growth.

> But if the Spirit of him that raised up Jesus from the dead dwell in you, he that raised up Christ from the dead shall also quicken your mortal bodies by his Spirit that dwelleth in you.

> Romans 8:11

Yes, Lord, yes. By Your Holy Spirit, come into my life today.

We need wisdom and knowledge. Wisdom gives knowledge. We can bring joy to God's heart by bearing genuine Christian fruit. Knowledge without wisdom makes one proud.

> to lead a life worthy of the Lord, fully pleasing to him, bearing fruit in every good work and increasing in the knowledge of God.
>
> Colossians 1:10 RSV

Lord, we want to live such a life. Thank You that You will lead us by Your Spirit.

When depression comes upon you, it is important to find the reason. It is the first step toward being free of the darkness which grips you. God will give His children a clear answer when they are willing to listen in obedience. Finding the reason for the darkness is in itself a work of liberation. And the darkness never needs to continue!

> The people that walked in darkness have seen a great light: they that dwell in the land of the shadow of death, upon them hath the light shined.
>
> Isaiah 9:2

Thank You, Father, that Your light shines into our darkness and that it is always stronger than the darkness.

May 27

There is no shortcut to holiness, and no detour.

> Follow . . . holiness, without which no man shall see the
> Lord: Looking diligently lest any man fail of the grace of
> God . . . .
>
> Hebrews 12:14, 15

Lord, make me more intent to follow holiness, that I may see You,
and make me watchful in all I do and say and think. Thank You,
that You are able.

May 28

There is a difference between intelligence and wisdom. Intelligence is of the earth; wisdom is a gift of God. Our senses give us
information about the world around us. The better a person handles
that which his senses convey to him, the more intelligent he is.
Wisdom is the gift to recognize God's presence in a certain situation and to act accordingly.

To the intelligent person, wisdom often seems foolish, because it
acts and thinks in a different way from that which intelligence may
demand. Intelligence gives outward prosperity; wisdom gives in-
ward peace. Intelligence is concerned with *this* world, wisdom with
the future world as well as this present world. That is why we can
pray for wisdom.

> Wisdom is the principal thing; therefore get wisdom . . . .
> Trust in the Lord with all thine heart; and lean not unto thine
> own understanding.
>
> Proverbs 4:7; 3:5

Lord, give us wisdom. We need it so very much. We want also to
be prepared for the future world—the world of eternity. Speak to
us and teach us.

May 29

Our work, also our service for God, can come between us and Christ if we do not realize that we are branches. Absolute dependence is the essence of the faith of the angels; it should also be ours. He is willing to do everything in us.

> . . . This is the work of God, that ye believe on him whom he hath sent.
>
> John 6:29

Lord, I believe in You. Help me to be more utterly dependent on You. Thank You that then You will glorify Yourself.

May 30

What God taught me when I was in the concentration camp, He is also willing to teach you. What did I learn? I learned how futile the things of the world are and how to conquer the things of the world in us. I learned to know the source of strength, and that this source is not in us, but in God.

> For with thee is the fountain of life . . . .
>
> Psalms 36:9

Teach each one of us, O Lord, the futility of the things of the world, that we may consider the things that are of Your Kingdom.

We can pray now that God will take away our fears when the moment of death comes. God always answers that prayer. Christians who prayed that prayer have had peaceful entrances into God's glory when they died. God is not weak, but strong. When you belong to Him, you are not weak, but strong. God's power is at your disposal through faith.

> But without faith it is impossible to please him: for he that cometh to God must believe that he is, and that he is a rewarder of them that diligently seek him.
>
> Hebrews 11:6

Lord, give me Your peace today, and tomorrow, and even the moment that I have to die.

JUNE

June 1

Harm and wounds inflicted by others can be so deep, the scars so painful, that humanly speaking it is impossible to forgive. But Jesus gave us God's love, and this love is always abundant. Did you, did I, really accept this love from Him?

> . . . God's love has been poured into our hearts through the Holy Spirit which has been given to us.
>
> Romans 5:5 RSV

Will you show me, Father, whether I really am willing to accept this love of Yours each time my own feelings are unloving? Make me willing to open my heart to Your love.

June 2

We cannot love one another too much. It is impossible to love too much. We cannot approach that, much less pass it, so we cannot love too much. Only let the love be selfless, strong, brave, faithful. There are always chances for strengthening one another's hands in God; let us not lose our chances.

AMY CARMICHAEL

> This is my commandment, That ye love one another, as I have loved you.
>
> John 15:12

Lord, You can give us this love. Please, do so today.

86

June 3

The source of love is not in ourselves. When Jesus tells us to love our enemies, He Himself will give us the love with which to do so. We are neither factories nor reservoirs of His love—only channels. When we understand that, all excuses for our lack of love are eliminated.

. . . love one another with a pure heart fervently.

1 Peter 1:22

Love through me, Lord.

June 4

Love's strength is evident in love's sacrifice. He who suffers most has most to give.

God's love is not something natural; it does not grow in our life's garden. The subject of Christian life is not man, but God. However, men are used as instruments of God.

. . . he who believes in me will also do the works that I do; and greater works than these will he do, because I go to the Father.

John 14:12 RSV

Make me an instrument that You can use, Lord.

June 5

Love is strong as death. Love is the only solution to the world's problems. The greatest demonstration of God's love for us was sending His only Son into the world to die for our sins in order to give us eternal life. We cannot use the name of Jesus if we do not walk in love. When we step out of love, the Bible is a closed book and our fellowship with the Father is broken. The Father's nature is love.

> I have loved you just as the Father has loved me. You must go on living in my love. If you keep my commandments you will live in my love just as I have kept my Father's commandments and live in his love. I have told you this so that you can share my joy, and that your joy may be complete.

> John 15:9–11 PHILLIPS

Lord, You know how often we fall short of this love of Yours although You tell us that it need not be so. Make us willing to keep Your commandments and live in Your love.

June 6

"Come to me *all*," Jesus says. That means that every communist may come, every prisoner in every prison. But how will they know if nobody tells them?

Are you telling them? Are you praying for the people who reach them and help them? Ask the Lord where He wants to use you

> . . . how shall they believe in him of whom they have not heard? . . .

> Romans 10:14

Thank You, Lord, that together with You, I can be the light of the world. We two will win.

June 7

How can we grow? Many think we grow through experience, and
that is true, but truer yet is the answer "by the Word." Don't forget
that it is God's Spirit who makes the Word alive to us.

> It is the spirit that gives life . . . the words that I have spoken
> to you are spirit and life.
>
> John 6:63 RSV

Lord, when I think of the last months, I must confess that there
was not much growth. Fill me with Your Holy Spirit, that Your
Word becomes more alive to me and that I see my experiences as
Your training.

June 8

I gave some talks at a university. One of the students knew he
had to make a decision. After the meeting, he went to the top of a
high mountain and cried aloud, "Lord Jesus Christ." After he had
done that for the third time, the Lord showed him some very practical things he had to do. Among those things was to burn a book by
a sect leader and to give a picture away. He gave the picture to me
and wrote his name on it with these words: "There was a great
celebration in heaven." I had said in my talk that the angels rejoice
when a sinner is saved.

It is true that we don't always have to go to a high mountain to
accept Jesus Christ as our Saviour, but everyone has to make a
decision for Jesus Christ, to become a child of God. Have you done
it yet? Did you take the next step and open your heart for the
fulness of the Holy Spirit? Jesus sent us the Comforter, and He is
willing to fill us to the utmost. Keep your heart clean by confessing
your sins to Jesus, and He will cleanse you with His blood. Then

the fruit of the Spirit will come, and He will make you a useful channel for streams of living water.

> . . . whoever drinks of the water that I shall give him will never thirst; the water that I shall give him will become in him a spring of water welling up to eternal life.
>
> John 4:14 RSV

O Lord, will You give the angels joy by saving me, a sinner?

June 9

I would very much like to teach you an important lesson. There was a time when they took away my Bible. Do you know what they could not take away? All the Scriptures I knew by heart. Why don't you start to collect Scriptures for times of trouble? Here are some that helped me:

> . . . whatever we may have to go through now is less than nothing compared with the magnificent future God has in store for us.
>
> Romans 8:18 PHILLIPS

> We pray that you will be strengthened from God's glorious power, so that you may be able to pass through any experience and endure it with joy.
>
> Colossians 1:11 PHILLIPS

Father, how great You are, willing to strengthen us from Your glorious power, enabling us to pass through any experience in order to bring glory to Your holy name.

June 10

When you read this text, there is a choice to make: perhaps for the first time, perhaps again. Is it "yes" or "yes, but"?

> For the wages of sin is death; but the gift of God is eternal life through Jesus Christ our Lord.
>
> Romans 6:23

Thank You, Lord, that I may choose.
Thank You, Lord, that I can depend on You.
Thank You, Lord, that I can know that what You said is true.

June 11

How about that book, the Bible? Throughout its sixty-six different yet unified divisions, the Bible claims for itself divine inspiration. It is accepted as the Word of God. Inspired but understandable, threatened but indestructible, it offers life to the believer, hope to the hopeless, and direction to all who trust its words.

> All scripture is given by inspiration of God, and is profitable for . . . instruction in righteousness.
>
> 2 Timothy 3:16

Holy Spirit, teach me to read the Bible. When You open my eyes and heart it makes me so rich.

June 12

Let us have done with whittling away the vast promises of the divine Word. Let these come within the limits of our poverty-stricken experience, and let us look unto Jesus, who is longing and willing to bring our experiences in accordance with God's promises.

> . . . Wherefore hearest thou men's words . . . ?
>
> 1 Samuel 24:9

> The eyes of your understanding being enlightened; that ye may know . . . .
>
> Ephesians 1:18

With our small human minds, we can never grasp the vast riches of eternity, Father. Yet You promised us the light of Your Spirit. We ask You today to give it to us in a greater measure.

June 13

Recently a thirteen-year-old girl sent me a small banner, on which she had very minutely embroidered two verses from Psalm 119, meant as an encouragement during the long time of recovery from my illness.

These were the words:

> Thy word is a lamp unto my feet, and a light unto my path . . . . Thou art my hiding place and my shield: I hope in thy word.
>
> Psalms 119:105, 114

Father, what a comfort that again and again we experience that Your Word indeed lightens our path whenever we cannot clearly see it. Help us to always hope in Your Word. Thank You that You are our hiding place and our shield.

June 14

The Bible is not like other books. It is the Word of God, the sword of the Spirit. We must handle it with reverence. When we read and teach it under the guidance of God's Spirit, it is a sharp sword.

> For the word of God is living and active, sharper than any two-edged sword, piercing to the division of soul and spirit, of joints and marrow, and discerning the thoughts and intentions of the heart.
>
> Hebrews 4:12 RSV

Our Father, You gave us Your Word to feed on it, to be strengthened by it, and to use it to show others the way to come to You. We thank You for all of this. But we ask You to make us willing to have our thoughts and intentions shown to us and then to do what You tell us to do.

June 15

The crisis in Bible study comes when we make the decision as to whether or not we accept the truth that has been revealed. The Old Testament is full of expectancy of what God will do; the New Testament looks back on the things God did. But both Old and New Testaments find fulfillment in the Lord Jesus Christ, who is the same Lord yesterday, today, and all the tomorrows.

> In the past God spoke to our forefathers through the prophets at many times and in various ways, but in these last days he has spoken to us by his Son . . . .
>
> Hebrews 1:1, 2 NIV

Thank You, Father, for giving us Your Word. Thank You for all it tells us of Your doings. Open our hearts and minds, that we may understand.

June 16

The power of the Gospel can cope with the lowest forms of heathenism and the worst superstitions. Oh, the power of the simple preaching of the Gospel!

> The times of ignorance God overlooked, but now he commands all men everywhere to repent.
>
> Acts 17:30 RSV

Our Father, we thank You that the message of the Gospel is so simple. Make us obedient to Your command that we should repent, and help us always to come to You at once with any sin, so that it cannot take root.

June 17

Knowledge is of no value until you know how to use it. Let the Holy Spirit lead you in the choice of study and reading.

> . . . your ears shall hear a word behind you, saying, This is the way . . . .
>
> Isaiah 30:21 RSV

I will listen in obedience, Lord. I will do Your will in Your strength.

June 18

Thank God for the battle verses in the Bible. We go into the unknown every day of our lives, and it is sure to be a battlefield, outwardly and evidently, or inwardly in that unseen life of the spirit, which is often by far the sternest battlefield for souls. . . .

AMY CARMICHAEL

> The Lord your God which goeth before you, he shall fight for you . . . .
>
> Deuteronomy 1:30

Father, we have so often experienced that You fight for us, that the battle is Yours. Help us to stand in Your strength this day, watching for that which You will do today.

June 19

Are you afraid of the end time, when those things shall happen which Jesus said would come on the earth before His return? You can trust Him to give you all you will need at that time. He will strengthen you, and He is the One to whom all power in heaven and on earth is given. Jesus said:

> . . . praying that you may be strong enough to come safely through all that is going to happen, and stand in the presence of the Son of Man.
>
> Luke 21:36 PHILLIPS

Thank You, Lord, that You will always be with us until the end of the world, and that You will never fail us nor forsake us. Thank You for this assurance.

The special task of God's children for this time is to be strong enough in the time of oppression. Is it possible that weak people can be ready for that? Yes. Everyone can be ready. I mean what I say: the Lord has given us all we need for the end time.

> But you are to be given power when the Holy Spirit has come to you. You will be witnesses to me. . . .
>
> Acts 1:8 PHILLIPS

Father, what peace there is in knowing that the Holy Spirit will prepare us and that You will perfect the work You began in us, till the day Jesus Christ arrives.

June 21

The end time has started already. Those who pay attention to the signs of the times will not doubt this at all. If we watch the events in the Middle East, in Israel, and in the Arab states, then we cannot do anything but look expectantly for the coming of the Lord. Every day, every hour, brings us nearer to His coming. We see many more signs of the times than ever before. It is the Lord's command that we observe the signs of the times. He said:

> Ye hypocrites, ye can discern the face of the sky and of the earth; but how is it that ye do not discern this time?
>
> Luke 12:56

> Watch therefore, for ye know neither the day nor the hour wherein the Son of man cometh.
>
> Matthew 25:13

Lord, will You open our eyes to discern the signs of this time? And, Lord, keep us watching.

June 22

So often people say to me "I cannot look forward with joy to the return of the Lord, because so many people are not converted yet." We see that things are getting worse and worse on earth. The unclean are getting more unclean. Today there are more lost ones than yesterday. Unbelief and lawlessness are increasing all over the world, not only outside the Church, but also in it.

For the Christian, Jesus' return will be the end of all battles, because our sanctification will then be accomplished completely.

> . . . that, when his glory shall be revealed, ye may be glad also with exceeding joy.
>
> 1 Peter 4:13

Lord, show me today where I can be used by You to save a soul for eternity.

June 23

There are many immature Christians. How often, after a meeting, I hear, "I will do my best to become a good Christian." Then I make it clear that becoming a child of God is a *present*, a matter first of all of taking what God gives in Christ. What a privilege that I can speak of the other foundation, not of feelings: "It is true, for it says so in the Bible."

> Then said they unto him, What shall we do, that we might work the works of God? Jesus answered and said unto them, This is the work of God, that ye believe on him whom he hath sent.
>
> John 6:28, 29

Father, I thank You that it is so simple; that You would have us just believe in Your Son, Jesus Christ. Help us, that we continually look unto Him, so that He may show us the Way.

Once I tried to help a pastor who was in great need. He said: "I feel . . . I hope . . . I shall do my best." I asked him if he wouldn't say: "It is true, for the Bible says so. I have accepted Jesus, and He gave me power to become a son of God."

His answer was: "If only I could be delivered from my training in the liberal university. If only I could see the Bible as you do." I told him that if we go to the Lord and tell Him all about our difficulties and ask Him to open our eyes to *see*, He will come and do so.

> If any of you lack wisdom, let him ask of God, that giveth to all men liberally . . . and it shall be given him.
>
> James 1:5

Heavenly Father, thank You for this promise in the Bible. Thank You that You will do all You have promised.

June 25

Knowing the future and understanding the present time do not need to make us downhearted, because the Lord has spoken many comforting words about the future.

> So likewise ye, when ye see these things come to pass, know ye that the kingdom of God is nigh at hand. . . . And when these things begin to come to pass, then look up, and lift up your heads; for your redemption draweth nigh. . . . But there shall not an hair of your head perish.
>
> Luke 21:31, 28, 18

Father, we thank You for all the comfort You give us in Your Word. We want to honor You by trusting You and rejoicing in You.

In the days before Jesus comes again, there will be greater stubbornness on the one side, but on the other side a deeper cleansing: either/or. Everything will reach a climax. Atheism is gaining ground, becoming more aggressive. The Kingdom of God continues to operate. It must be either Christ or anti-Christ; nobody can serve two masters.

> . . . the time is at hand. He that is unjust, let him be unjust still: and he which is filthy, let him be filthy still: and he that is righteous, let him be righteous still: and he that is holy, let him be holy still.
>
> Revelation 22:10, 11

Lord, open my eyes through Your Holy Spirit to what it means to live now and to be a Christian who knows that Jesus is coming soon.

If we pay heed to what happens in this world, to things that we look upon as signs that Jesus will come back very soon, we feel frightened when we consider what the Bible says about the time of anti-Christ. Awful things are going to happen then. Also, the moment in which we shall all have to appear before a righteous God will come. In order to be ready for these events, we need the many promises of the Bible.

> Heaven and earth shall pass away: but my words shall not pass away.
>
> Luke 21:33

Lord Jesus, we thank You that all the promises of the Bible find their fulfillment in You and that we can trust You at all times, knowing that the day of redemption will come.

June 28

If I were not a Christian, I would be very pessimistic. Because man has given himself to the devil and his service, the whole world lies in evil. How can we get out of this chaos? We must return to God's original plan. We can never change chaos. God can, and He does! We can read it in His Word.

> At various times in the past and in various different ways, God spoke to our ancestors . . . but in our own time, the last days. he has spoken to us through his Son . . . .
>
> Hebrews 1:1, 2 JERUSALEM

Father, we thank You that, right from the beginning of creation, You had Your plan for restoration. Thank You for speaking to us again and again. Give us ears to hear

June 29

If God should never again send any trials intended to point us and others to Him, would all our sufferings cease? No. Left to ourselves, with our sinful natures unchecked, greater harm would result. But as it is, He gives us only that which works for good and which will bring us closer to Him. And there is something else: If we know Him as our Lord and Saviour, we will, at His time, go to heaven, where we will never suffer again.

> . . . I reckon that the sufferings of this present time are not worthy to be compared with the glory which shall be revealed in us.
>
> Romans 8:18

Father, thank You that all that comes our way is permitted by Your love. Although we know it, we so often forget. Please, remind us again and again. We praise You for Your love, which is behind it all.

I heard someone say, "I don't believe in Jesus' coming again. So many have prophesied, and nothing happened."

I answered him, "You are one of the signs of the time, for Peter told us that such sayings belonged to the conversation of the last days."

> Knowing this first, that there shall come in the last days scoffers . . . saying, Where is the promise of his coming? . . .
>
> 2 Peter 3:3, 4

Lord, make me, through Your Holy Spirit, a positive witness of the prophecies and set a watch for my lips, that the enemy cannot make me spread unbelief.

JULY

July 1

How you and I behave is important for the great end battle in which we might be already engaged.

This will be a time for you to bear testimony.

Luke 21:13 RSV

Lord, take my weak hand in Your strong one, so that together we can stand on victory ground.

July 2

How the world, with its turmoil and problems of this time, needs Christians who are willing to speak up! After all, we are the only ones in the whole world who know the future and who can understand our present days. Because this knowledge is depressing, the Lord comforts us regarding these days:

. . . for the elect's sake those days shall be shortened.

Matthew 24:22

Thank You, Lord, that we know that You have plans, not problems, and that there is never a panic in heaven.

July 3

Here is something which helps me when I am discouraged because of sin:

> When Satan tempts me to despair
> And tells me of my sins within,
> Upwards I look and see Him there
> Who made an end of all my sin.

Will you not try to see what looking to Jesus will do for you?

> Looking unto Jesus the author and finisher of our faith . . . .
> consider him that endured such contradiction of sinners
> against himself, lest ye be wearied and faint in your minds.
>
> Hebrews 12:2, 3

Lord Jesus, thank You that, when we look to You, You will strengthen us, as our Father strengthened You.

July 4

God made His plan for this world known unto us. It is His will that the history of mankind will find its fulfillment in Jesus and that all things in heaven and on earth will be made perfect in Him.

And the overwhelming part of it is that Jesus promised to share everything which is His with us.

> Father, I will that they also, whom thou hast given me, be with
> me where I am; that they may behold my glory, which thou
> hast given me . . . .
>
> John 17:24

Lord Jesus, we cannot fully grasp what it means to behold Your glory. But we thank You that one day we shall understand.

July 5

God has hidden the day of Jesus' coming again in order that we may be ready every day, watching our daily walk and actions.

> But we are citizens of Heaven; we eagerly wait for the saviour . . . .
>
> Philippians 3:20 PHILLIPS

Lord Jesus, thank You for introducing us to the Father. Thank You that we are citizens of heaven and children of our Father in heaven.

July 6

Cross bearing, as a form of martyrdom, has become unknown in the Western world; in the Eastern world it has not. Nevertheless, it is of great importance nowadays, for the opposition against God and the cross is increasing.

> That day will not come before there first arises a definite rejection of God and the appearance of the lawless man. He is the product of all that leads to death, and he sets himself up in opposition to every religion.
>
> 2 Thessalonians 2:3, 4 PHILLIPS

Lord, prepare us for the days when anti-Christ will reveal himself. Make us able to withstand and to stand against the wiles of the devil.

July 7

Before Jesus returns, there will be a hard battle. Therefore it is good to prepare ourselves for battle with His strength. Every Christian is called to take his place in the army of King Jesus and to wrestle as a fellow conqueror together with Him.

> For we wrestle not against flesh and blood, but against principalities, against powers . . . against spiritual wickedness in high places.
>
> Ephesians 6:12

Lord Jesus, I belong to You, and therefore You also call me to take my place in Your army. Thank You that I know that You are the Victor.

July 8

Everyone on this earth is expecting—and many are fearing—another war. This war will be ended with such a display of divine intervention that a great many of the surviving Gentiles and Jews will put their whole trust in Jesus, the Messiah.

> . . . We have found the Messias . . . .
>
> John 1:41

Father, Your plan for this earth and for its inhabitants is perfect. And we know that You will fulfill it. Thank You for all who have accepted Your Son as their Saviour and Lord, and for all who will do so.

Every promise in the Bible is *yes* and *amen* in Jesus. I have seen—and I know it is true—when reading the Bible, that it says very clearly that the Lord Jesus Himself will prepare us for that great day when we shall see Him face-to-face. I do long for His coming. Do you?

. . . Even so, come, Lord Jesus.

Revelation 22:20

Thank You, Lord, for taking our hands in Yours, holding us, and strengthening us every day anew, until that day when we shall see You face-to-face. Hallelujah!

July 10

As long as there is fear in our hearts, we will never understand what God is saying. It took Jacob many years to understand, but we do not need such a long time. Jesus has conquered our fears.

. . . Fear not; I am the first and the last.

Revelation 1:17

Thank You, Lord, that You are from everlasting to everlasting, so that we never need fear. Keep our eyes on You.

July 11

Are you feeling discouraged today? Or are you passing through a time of real distress? Will you let me share with you what has helped me so often?

> He that dwelleth in the secret place of the most High shall abide under the shadow of the Almighty. I will say of the Lord, He is my refuge and my fortress: my God; in him will I trust. . . . He shall cover thee with his feathers, and under his wings shalt thou trust: his truth shall be thy shield and buckler.
>
> Psalms 91:1, 2, 4

Father, please, speak to all who are feeling discouraged. Perhaps by these words, perhaps in another way, let them know You are always near to each one of them. May Your presence give them joy.

July 12

Are you seeking happiness? Is that your only goal? We set our minds on something we think will make us happy—a husband, children, a particular job, or even a ministry—and refuse to open our eyes to God's better way. In fact, there are those who believe so strongly that only this one thing can bring happiness that they reject the Lord Jesus Himself.

Happiness is not found in marriage, or work, or ministry, or children, in themselves. Happiness is found in being secure in Jesus, in obedience to Him, in doing His will. Then we have fellowship with Him and we can speak to Him about everything that occupies our thoughts, and all these other things find their proper places in His plan for our lives.

We know that God does not listen to sinners. He listens to the godly man who does his will.

John 9:31 NIV

Father, You know which way is best. I do not want to choose for myself how my life is going to be. What mistakes I would make! Make me willing to listen to You and to obey You.

July 13

The will of God is either a burden we carry or a power which carries us.

. . . All power is given unto me in heaven and in earth.

Matthew 28:18

Lord, I surrender my will to You.

July 14

All our failings, as Christians and Christian nations, do not change the fact that Jesus is the Way and that through Him only can we come to the living God.

Neither is there salvation in any other: for there is none other name under heaven given among men, whereby we must be saved.

Acts 4:12

Lord, set my feet on victory ground. Forgive me that I sought the way that was wrong. Lead me in the right path.

Prosperity can cause superficiality, and that is a danger. Having every corner of our lives under the control of God means victory. Again and again, a total surrender is necessary, and then we experience that *all* things, also prosperity, work together for good.

> I know . . . both to abound and to suffer need.
>
> Philippians 4:12

Lord, have I money? Or has the money me? Make me a faithful ambassador of heaven.

When we seek the Lord's guidance, we must have nothing to do with other forms of guidance. He will guide us by His Spirit if we ask Him to do so, if we are submissive to Him and refuse to be led by our own wishes.

> So the Lord alone did lead him, and there was no strange god with him.
>
> Deuteronomy 32:12

Thank You, Lord, that we can leave everything to You, because You know best. Make us willing each day to submit all our wishes, thoughts, and desires to You. Your will be done.

July 17

It seems to be God's plan to allow all sorts of things to happen, that would naturally cause fear, but to forestall them by the assurance of His presence.

AMY CARMICHAEL

And the Lord, he it is that doth go before thee; he will be with thee, he will not fail thee, neither forsake thee: fear not, neither be dismayed.

Deuteronomy 31:8

You know, Father, how much we need You this day. Thank You that Your Word stands forever. Thank You that You are going before us during this whole day.

July 18

Do you know how it feels when you are dead tired? Sometimes I feel like that. One day I spoke about it to the Lord. He showed me that it was wrong to feel irritated; that it was sin. I began to argue, until I remembered that Jesus cannot cleanse excuses. Then I confessed my sin and told the Lord I was willing to do whatever He wanted me to do. My joy became very deep when I read:

When I think of the wisdom and scope of his plan I fall down on my knees and pray to the Father of all the great family of God . . . that out of his glorious, unlimited resources he will give you the mighty inner strengthening of his Holy Spirit. And I pray that Christ will be more and more at home in your hearts, living within you as you trust in him. May your roots go down deep into the soil of God's marvelous love; and may you be able to feel and understand, as all God's children should, how long, how wide, how deep, and how high his love really is; and to experience this love for yourselves, though it is so great that you will never see the end of it or fully know or understand it. And so at last you will be filled up with God himself.

Ephesians 3:14–19 LB

It encouraged me to know and to trust that the limitless resources of His strength are more than sufficient. I began to praise the Lord and to thank Him. My tiredness disappeared.

And today also I praise and thank You, Lord. You will give me the strength I need for this day.

July 19

There are times when we cannot depend on anything but God. Then we must be in perfect union with Him. Get in training. Practice depending on your heavenly Father in your everyday life.

> And they that know thy name will put their trust in thee: for thou, Lord, hast not forsaken them that seek thee.
>
> Psalms 9:10

Father, You know that I trust in You. Yet at times it seems as if You are far away. Show me in what respect I depend on somebody or something else, instead of on You only. I know You will always be with me, if I remain close to You. Hallelujah!

July 20

We know that on the cross of Calvary all was finished that had to be done to prepare us for the future. Jesus said, "It is finished." And when we look at Calvary's Cross, we know it is Jesus who calls us.

> I came not to call the righteous, but sinners to repentance.
>
> Luke 5:32

Lord, we thank You that *You* are calling us. You know how weak we feel in ourselves, how we never can become blameless and holy by trying. But, oh, we thank You that You did all that had to be done and that we just have to accept it from You.

The well-known American missionary to India E. Stanley Jones tells of an experience he once had: "One day I watched an eagle in the Himalayas face a storm. I wondered what the eagle would do as the storm rushed through the narrow valley. Would it fly above the fury of the storm? Would it be dashed to pieces on the rocks below? No! It set its wings in such a way that the air current sent him above the storm with its fury. He used the storm to reach greater heights."

We must learn this lesson of turning all resistance into opportunities of release. Then we shall know how to live. With the eagle it was a setting of wings that made the difference. For us it is saying yes to God.

> . . . choose you this day whom ye will serve . . . .
>
> Joshua 24:15

Yes, Lord, I want to serve You. Thank You that it is possible to turn that which seems to be a hindrance into something that will glorify You.

We sit with Christ on His throne as soon as we have surrendered all our crowns and made Him sole and only ruler of our life and its possessions.

> [God has] raised us up with him, and made us sit with him in the heavenly places in Christ Jesus.
>
> Ephesians 2:6 RSV

Yes, Lord, forgive my "yes, buts."

July 23

When we are obedient, God guides our steps and our stops. Beware of shortcuts in guidance; it is far better to take a detour with Him than shortcuts without Him.

. . . the Lord thy God is he which goeth over before thee . . . .

Deuteronomy 9:3

For the Lord thy God bringeth thee into a good land, a land of brooks of water, of fountains and depths that spring out of valleys and hills.

Deuteronomy 8:7

Forgive me, Lord, my shortcuts. Take my whole life.

July 24

When your will differs from God's will, what are you going to do?

[*Jesus* said] . . . not my will, but thine, be done.

Luke 22:42

Lord, make us like-minded with You, that we can also say from our hearts: Father, Your will be done. You know best.

July 25

Wherever I go, I find Christians needing encouragement. In these days so full of darkness, chaos, and hopelessness, it is dangerous to live as a Christian who has stopped halfway. We have the great responsibility of being the light of the world.

You are the light of the world . . . .

Matthew 5:14 RSV

Lord, You know that in ourselves we have no light, but we thank You that You let Your light shine through us, that others may see.

If you say no to God at any point, you have allied yourself with the evil forces which are in rebellion against God. To whom do you listen—to God or to the devil? It is either/or.

> Whom hast thou reproached and blasphemed? and against whom hast thou exalted thy voice, and lifted up thine eyes on high? even against the Holy One of Israel.
>
> Isaiah 37:23

Father, cause us to realize what it means if we say no to You. So often we are not willing to submit. Forgive us and make us strong in Your power.

Satan sometimes suggests that a money offering will satisfy God, when in fact He is demanding our all. Losing our life for Jesus' sake is one inescapable requirement. But how great is our gain! We are the great losers when we persuade ourselves that the giving of money is sufficient. Jesus gave His life for you and me. Shall we then not give our lives to Him, letting go of our own wishes and desires?

> Whoever seeks to gain his life will lose it, but whoever loses his life will preserve it.
>
> Luke 17:33 RSV

Lord, take my life and use it in Your service.

July 28

Those who are not willing to obey the Lord can never understand what He is saying. Only those who are willing to obey what God reveals to them can be effectively instructed.

> . . . To know wisdom and instruction . . . . but fools despise wisdom and instruction.
>
> Proverbs 1:2, 7

How wonderful it is, Lord, that You are willing to instruct us and that it is possible for us to understand *and* to obey.

July 29

When we really rely on the Holy Spirit, He will guide us. We from our side must fulfill one important condition: obedience.

> . . . I being in the way, the Lord led me . . . .
>
> Genesis 24:27

Thank You, Father, that You are always willing to lead us, if only we are willing to obey and remain in Your way.

July 30

Each time we put our hand in His and go on through life together with Him, we may ask Him to lead us till our last day on this earth comes. We cannot go alone—not one step—but "Lord, take me with You wherever You go." We can ask Him to let us rest at His feet. Isn't that wonderful?

In ourselves we are so poor, but in Him we are rich—in Him who said He would make us more than conquerors. Then we do not need to fear the future. He will lead us on the narrow pathway.

. . . in every thing ye are enriched by him. . . . .

1 Corinthians 1:5

Lord, we thank You that we do not need to worry, but that You will guide us, even in these very serious times. And not only that, Lord, but You want to make us witnesses of Yourself in a world so full of darkness. Will You make us lights in the world? Thank You, Lord.

July 31

The person who trusts God, but with restrictions, is like a wave of the sea driven to and fro by the wind. He cannot expect to receive anything from God. The life of such a one, who only trusts God in part, is unstable in every respect.

> Commit thy way unto the Lord; trust also in him; and he shall bring it to pass.

Psalms 37:5

Lord, we want to commit our whole lives, also the smallest details, to You, not being tossed about like the waves of the sea. Help us to continually look up to You.

AUGUST

August 1

We have the privilege of being co-workers with God. Perhaps you say, "I am weak," or "I am old, what can I do?" But the Lord is not weak. He is building His Kingdom. We are only His co-workers.

Surrender and obedience, willingness to work where He thinks it necessary—that is what He is asking from us. Then we stand on victory ground, and the Lord will use us and make us channels for the streams of living water, wherever we may work. Hallelujah!

. . . All that the Lord hath said will we do, and be obedient.

Exodus 24:7

. . . we are labourers together with God . .

1 Corinthians 3:9

Thank You, Father, for the privilege of being co-workers with You. Make us faithful and always willing for whatever You want us to do.

Whatever happens, be sure that your everyday life is honoring to the Lord. Then you will have power, and your life will point others to Him.

> And God is able to make all grace abound toward you . . . .
>
> 2 Corinthians 9:8

Lord, let Your grace be seen in my everyday life.

You who are God's children, are you only occupied with yourselves, rejoicing in what the Lord did for you? Or are you concerned about the many, just within reach, who do not know Jesus yet? Perhaps you feel inadequate as to how to tell them of the great love of Jesus for them. Just ask the Lord to let His Holy Spirit show you the needs of those around you. He will give you the opportunities and the right words to speak to them of Him.

> But exhort one another every day, as long as it is called "today," that none of you may be hardened by the deceitfulness of sin.
>
> Hebréws 3:13 RSV

Lord, I want to tell others of You. Lead me by Your Spirit to those who long for You and give me the right words to point them to You and to Your love for sinners. Grant that they may repent and come to You.

August 4

There are two sorts of failures: those that think and do not do, and those that do and do not think. This may seem an exaggeration, yet both kinds of people exist. Are you one of them? If so, ask the Lord to show you how to combine the thinking and the doing so that there are no contradictions in your life. Don't forget: people watch you, and they want to see Jesus.

> But the mercy of the Lord is . . . upon them that fear him, and his righteousness . . . to those that remember his commandments to do them.
>
> Psalms 103:17, 18

Father, help us to remember Your commandments and to do them, living according to Your will with great joy, that others may know it is You, working in us in all we think and do.

August 5

The more you walk with the Lord, the more He will increase your strength and enable you to do His work. The more you do God's will, the better you will discern what His will is.

> . . . that you may be filled with the knowledge of his will in all spiritual wisdom and understanding.
>
> Colossians 1:9 RSV

Yes, Father, it is the desire of my heart to do Your will and to walk with You. Thank You that You are always willing to strengthen and encourage me and that Your riches are inexhaustible.

The Lord always gives grace for just this day. I must not live in the future or in the past, but just today—today with Him. This is the day of the Lord.

. . . Be still, for the day is holy . . . .

Nehemiah 8:11 NAS

Help me, Lord, to live one day at a time. Thank You that Your grace is sufficient for today and that I don't need to worry about tomorrow, because Your grace will be sufficient for tomorrow also.

The Lord God is the One who gives life, and who gives us the life of eternity when we accept Jesus Christ as our Saviour and Lord. We live because of His infinite grace. He makes us strong. He shows us the way in which we must serve Him, and His hand is guiding us along that way.

O Lord . . . . Be our arm every morning . . . .

Isaiah 33:2 RSV

Lead us, Father, along the paths You choose for us, whatever they may be. Help us to realize every day that You do not slumber or sleep and that You will not let our feet slip. We thank You for Your wisdom in leading us.

August 8

Our real songs begin with our sacrifices. We enter the realm of music when we enter the realm of self-surrender. A willing offering on a clean altar introduces the soul into "the joy of the Lord."

> . . . when the burnt offering began, the song of the Lord began also . . . .
>
> 2 Chronicles 29:27

O Lord, a clean altar—a willing offering—is what You expect, and it is the desire of our hearts. Let us never forget that we enter into Your holy presence when we bring an offering.

August 9

One day, when he was old, Francis of Assisi was asked how it was possible he did so much for God. His answer was: "The reason that God blessed my endeavors must have been this: God looked down from heaven and said, 'Where can I find the weakest, lowliest, poorest man on earth?' Then He saw me and He said: 'I found him. I will work through him, for surely it will not cause him to think anything of himself and take My glory to be his. He will know that I always used him, just because he was lowly and did not think himself important.' "

> . . . God chose what is foolish in the world to shame the wise, God chose what is weak in the world to shame the strong, God chose what is low and despised in the world . . . to bring to nothing things that are, so that no human being might boast in the presence of God.
>
> 1 Corinthians 1:27–29 RSV

Father, if You will, You can use even me. Make me willing to be looked upon as foolish by the world, if people should consider me so.

Once there was an old monk who sang a Christmas song every Christmas Eve. His voice was ugly, but he loved the Lord and sang from his heart. One day the head of the cloister said, "I'm sorry, Brother Don, we have a new monk with a beautiful voice . . . . he will sing this Christmas." The man sang so beautifully that everyone was happy.

But that night an angel came to the superior and said; "Why didn't you have a Christmas Eve song?"

The superior answered, "We had a beautiful song."

But the angel said sadly "We did not hear it in heaven."

You see, the old monk had a personal relationship with the Lord Jesus, but the young man sang for his own benefit, not for the Lord's glory.

> . . . whatsoever ye do, do all to the glory of God.
>
> 1 Corinthians 10:31

Lord, self slips in so easily, when all I want is to do things for Your glory. Let me always hear the voice of Your Holy Spirit.

Many church members may be working hard and yet, when they go to heaven, their hands may be empty because they never won a soul for Christ. They have nothing to offer as a token of gratitude. They are like the disciples, who after Christ had died and risen again, went back to their fishing. They fished all night and did not catch one fish.

Is that not the life of many Christians? They try so hard, they study so hard, and yet end up without having anything with eternal value.

For we are his workmanship, created in Christ Jesus for good works, which God prepared beforehand, that we should walk in them.

Ephesians 2:10 RSV

Open our eyes, Father, to the fact that we have to step into doing the works You ordained for us to walk in. And we thank You that You will show us what these works are.

August 12

When all securities and riches and values of the world crumble and fall away, you will experience the indestructible riches of God's promises.

. . . the world passes away, and the lust of it; but he who does the will of God abides for ever.

1 John 2:17 RSV

Lord, Your Word says that it is possible to abide in You, which means that we shall always be where You are. Then we shall see the fulfillment of Your promises. Hallelujah!

August 13

When I was in solitary confinement, I wrote in one of my letters, "I long for freedom, but I hope I will not lose the joyful consciousness of Jesus' presence that I have here in this cell." Do you also know what it means to feel the presence of Jesus? There is nothing that can surpass it. And He Himself promised that He would be with us!

> . . . I am with you alway, even unto the end of the world . . . .
>
> Matthew 28:20

Thank You, Lord, that we shall never be left to ourselves, because You are always with us. How privileged we are!

August 14

Jesus is the great turning point in the history of mankind and creation. He was the first of whom God said, "He is My beloved Son." Till then every man in the Bible and in history had had his limitations and weaknesses. Jesus had God's very own nature. If we want to know God, we must study the life of Jesus.

> Therefore, holy brethren, who share in a heavenly call, consider Jesus, the apostle and high priest of our confession.
>
> Hebrews 3:1 RSV

Father, we thank You that You gave Your only Son and made it possible for mankind—for each one of us—to partake of His life if we accept Him as Saviour and Lord. We want to keep close to Him. Help us to do so.

August 15

Jesus is God's armor! He is truth, righteousness, peace, faith, salvation.

> . . . I am the way, the truth, and the life . . . .
>
> John 14:6

> Neither is there salvation in any other . . . .
>
> Acts 4:12

Father, we can never thank You enough for the wonderful provision You made for us in Your Son, Jesus Christ. Teach us to accept it anew every day.

August 16

Who is that source of defense, that Helper in whom you and I must trust? It is the Lord of lords, it is the King of kings.

> . . . he hath said, I will never leave thee, nor forsake thee. So that we may boldly say, The Lord is my helper, and I will not fear what man shall do unto me.
>
> Hebrews 13:5, 6

O Lord, what a strong and loving heavenly Father You are. Thank You that I may lay my trembling hand in Your strong one.

August 17

The wells of the Lord are to be found when I most need them.

John Henry Jowett wrote: "There was a farmer who for a generation had carried every pail of water from a distant well to meet the need of his homestead. One day he sunk a shaft by his own house, and to his great joy, he found that the water was waiting at his own gate.

"My soul, your well is near, even here. Go not in search of Him. Your pilgrimage is ended: the waters are at your feet."

> He sendeth the springs into the valleys . . . .
>
> Psalms 104:10

Lord Jesus, I make it so complicated. Make me, through Your Holy Spirit, as simple as a child, so that I live as rich as I am in You.

August 18

The possibilities of man are boundless indeed, but only if he does not put God's promises within boundaries. The Lord's words are full of the power of eternity and unshakeable. And these words of the Lord tell us that He has come very near to us. The presence of the Lord is our great comfort. He promised:

">. . . I am with you always, to the close of the age."

Matthew 28:20 RSV

Thank You, Father, that I am safe in the hands of Jesus.

August 19

The Lord Jesus knows all about you and me. He says, "I know My sheep." We do not take Him by surprise. He does not come in late and find the performance half-over. He is in at our beginnings

And thou shalt remember all the way which the Lord thy God led thee . . . in the wilderness . . . .

Deuteronomy 8:2

You know me, Lord—me! What a security!

August 20

Pray regularly, but also when you have to make a decision or when you have to resist a temptation. You can be in contact with God every moment. And He always hears you.

One thing have I desired of the Lord, that will I seek after; that I may dwell in the house of the Lord all the days of my life, to behold the beauty of the Lord, and to enquire in his temple.

Psalms 27:4

Thank You, Lord, that I can always be near to You and that I can go to You with any request. Above all, thank You that You are always willing to listen. Hallelujah!

126

Often we do not understand God's promises. They seem too lofty and beyond our comprehension, and so we lay them aside without really giving them serious thought. But that is not God's intention.

He backs every promise with His love and His omnipotence, and He was in earnest when He made them. Therefore I believe that we are sinning when we ignore them or perhaps evade them by explaining them away.

> We do not want any of you to grow slack, but to follow the example of those who through sheer patient faith came to possess the promises.
>
> Hebrews 6:12 PHILLIPS

And I do not want to grow slack, Lord. Make me more conscious of Your love, which gives me Your sure promise to strengthen and encourage me.

August 22

Often people ask me, "Why do I not hear God's answer? When I ask for guidance, it is as if the Lord is not willing to answer."

My answer then can only be a question: "Do you honestly expect an answer?" And they admit they don't.

> Acquaint now thyself with him, and be at peace. . . .
>
> Job 22:21

Lord, forgive and cleanse my fruitless prayer life. I see that I did not expect and did not wait. Thank You that You are a patient, understanding Teacher.

No one but yourself can rob you of the fulness of blessing. No man is deprived of any spiritual gift because of the failings and faults of others. Aaron's rod budded, blossomed, and gave fruit, even when tied up with a bundle of dry sticks.

> . . . the rod of Aaron was among their rods. And Moses laid up the rods before the Lord in the tabernacle of witness.
>
> Numbers 17:6, 7

If only we would always come to You, Lord, with all our thoughts, concerns, and longings and let You do what You think right. Make us more willing to come.

Never be ashamed of asking, seeking, and knocking at the storehouse of God's omnipotence. When we admit our helplessness to meet needs, we are expressing our dependence on God. That is the faith that moves mountains.

> . . . How long are ye slack to go to possess the land, which the Lord God . . . hath given you?
>
> Joshua 18:3

Forgive us, Lord, that so often we only look at our own poor resources, forgetting You are *the* Source. Help us to go and possess that which You have already given us.

Let us always be filled with holy discontentment regarding ourselves. We can never be sure of our own wishes, but we can of God's promises.

> He will keep you steadfast in the faith to the end, so that when his day comes you need fear no condemnation.
>
> 1 Corinthians 1:8 PHILLIPS

Thank You, Lord, that Your promises stand forever and that You will keep us steadfast, because Your promises never fail.

It is not so important *what* we experience as *how* we experience difficulties.

> How we thank God for all of this! It is he who makes us victorious through Jesus Christ our Lord!
>
> 1 Corinthians 15:57 LB

Lord, nevertheless I am continually with You, although Your way is hidden from me. I know You uphold me with Your right hand. You lead me according to Your counsel, even when I see nothing but darkness. You make a path in the wilderness and cause me to reach the goal. Lord, I am ashamed that I was so defeated. Help me to realize Your sustaining presence is always there.

In Hollywood I saw many different kinds of hands and faces and situations. I saw the hands of those who desired to be "Queen for a Day"—greedy, nervous, desperate hands. I saw folded hands of young boys and girls praying silently. I saw bored, unhappy faces. I saw happy young faces of boys and girls witnessing to the peace Jesus had brought into their hearts. I saw poverty—poignant poverty—in luxurious buildings. I saw the heavenly riches of God's children.

One was "Queen for a Day"—just one day.

Those who know Jesus are royal children for time and eternity. The world says, "One is allowed to come." Jesus says, "Come unto Me, *all*."

> . . . I am come that they might have life, and that they might have it more abundantly.

> John 10:10

O Lord, we never can fully grasp what it means that You were willing to come to this earth to suffer and die that we might have abundant life. Thank You, that You came for each one of us.

It is through Jesus that God's greatest and most precious promises have become available to us.

> O the depth of the riches and wisdom and knowledge of God! . . .

> Romans 11:33 RSV

It is a marvel to us, Father, that we are allowed to draw from Your Word and that the riches of Your promises are at our disposal. We thank You and praise Your holy name!

How rich I am! God is the Creator of the whole universe, yet is holding my life in His hands. He ever guides the constellations of stars, and at the same time remembers man. Wind and water also obey Him. And this is *my* God, *my* Father. I am His child. Nobody is like this Lord, and He loves me. How rich I am!

He . . . hangeth the earth upon nothing.

Job 26:7

What is man, that thou art mindful of him? . . . .

Psalms 8:4

Thank You, Lord, that You also have me in Your hand.

Do you know there is a difference between life and abundant life? Many Christians say, "I believe in Jesus; that is all I need. I have eternal life, so why these problems about abundant life?"

Once I saw a very sick person who could hardly move. Then a nurse entered the room. She was full of energy and strength, and came to help. Both had life. One just had life, the other had *abundant* life.

Too many Christians are like the sick person. They have life, yes, but they are not strong and cannot help others.

since you desire proof that Christ is speaking in me. He is not weak in dealing with you, but is powerful in you.

2 Corinthians 13:3 RSV

Thank You, Lord, that it is possible to live the abundant life, because it is You who are powerful, even in me.

God wants us to be independent of any bottle and to be abundantly satisfied with the well of water within us: a well fed from the hills of God.

> Understanding is a wellspring of life unto him that hath it
> . . . . the wellspring of wisdom as a flowing brook.

> Proverbs 16:22; 18:4

Lord, lead us into Your wisdom and let it be a well of water in us, not only for our own refreshment, but also for that of others.

SEPTEMBER

September 1

Do you know that God wants you to take Him at His Word? When we think about the dark days in which we live or about ourselves and our continual need of grace, strength, and guidance, we must always remember that God's promises are waiting for us, to meet our need. We do not need to say much, we only have to take Him at His Word. And He will give us rest.

. . . do as thou hast said.

2 Samuel 7:25

Father, You will never break Your Word. We know that You will always do as You have said. Thank You for Your Word and Your promises.

September 2

God's promises are spoken with full authority. You never come across any idle word in the Bible. Whatever God says, He means.

. . . the word of the Lord stands forever.

1 Peter 1:25 NIV

Thank You, Lord, for the sure foundation we have in Your Word.

133

September 3

Sometimes people start saying to me, "I feel that . . . ." What a privilege that I can speak of the truth, not of feelings. "It is true, for it says so in the Bible."

> For the law was given by Moses, but grace and truth came by Jesus Christ.
>
> John 1:17

Father, help us that we continually look unto Your Son, so that He may show us the way.

September 4

However poor and small and incomplete the faith of the disciples was, many times they had sufficient faith to make them do the right thing. When they were agitated and distressed, alarmed and exhausted, they went to Jesus, and He gave them all they needed.

> . . . Lord, to whom shall we go? You have the words of eternal life.
>
> John 6:68 RSV

> I am the bread of life.
>
> John 6:48 RSV

We say with Peter: "Lord, to whom shall we go?" You alone can fulfill our deepest needs. Thank You, that we can go to You at all times.

September 5

Are you concerned about the security of your faith? The reality of our redemption lies in the finished work of the Lord Jesus Christ at the cross, not in our own feelings and emotions. Feelings come and feelings go, but Jesus is always present.

> . . . that Christ may dwell in your hearts through faith; that you, being rooted and grounded in love, may have power . . . .
>
> Ephesians 3:17, 18 RSV

Lord, I can never thank You enough that at the cross You did all that was necessary to free me from the power of sin. Thank You that it is possible to have power, if I only remain rooted in love—in Your love.

September 6

Faith is an activity; it is something that has to be applied. Let us always be prepared to do so at the place and time of need or testing. Our faith is in God. He is the All-Sufficient One. By an act of will, we can always turn to Him.

> Let us therefore come boldly unto the throne of grace, that we may . . . find grace to help in time of need.
>
> Hebrews 4:16

Father, thank You that whenever we come to You, trusting and believing Your promises, we may come boldly. And thank You that in every need we shall find the grace which will help us just then.

September 7

Faith is important because it takes me to the Lord. It may be necessary for Him to rebuke me, but He will also receive me. He will give me a greater conception of Himself than I had before.

> Examine yourselves, whether ye be in the faith; prove your own selves . . . .
>
> 2 Corinthians 13:5

Lord, I thank You for all You have done in me ever since I came to You. Make me willing to examine myself, and to be corrected.

September 8

Faith is not anti-intellectual. It is an act of man that reaches beyond the limits of our five senses.

> Now faith is being sure of what we hope for and certain of what we do not see.
>
> Hebrews 11:1 NIV

Lord, we know our senses were given to us to use for the things of this earth. Faith has to do with the Kingdom of heaven. Thank You that what is impossible to man, is possible to You.

September 9

I have been thinking of how many unexplained things there are in life. Our Lord Jesus who could have explained everything, explained nothing. He said there would be tribulation, but He never said why. Sometimes He spoke of suffering being to the glory of God, but He never said how. All through the Scriptures it is the same. I cannot recall a single explanation of trial. Can you? We are trusted with the Unexplained.

AMY CARMICHAEL

That the trial of your faith, being much more precious than of gold that perisheth . . . might be found unto praise and honour and glory at the appearing of Jesus Christ.

1 Peter 1:7

Lord, strengthen us to live in patience and steadfastness, in every little call upon faith, as well as in every great call.

September 10

Because victory is the result of Christ's life lived out in the believer, it is important that we clearly see that victory, not defeat, is God's purpose for His children.

. . . Death is swallowed up in victory.

1 Corinthians 15:54

Thank You, Lord, for Your victory! Thank You that You are able—always!

September 11

We do not need to agree with each other about all the doctrines, but we must be able to discern the spirits. The Holy Spirit equips us with the gift of discernment. In these days many will try to deceive us. We must clearly discern what comes to us from the Holy Spirit and what is from the devil.

For false Christs shall arise, and false prophets, and will do wonderful miracles, so that if it were possible, even God's chosen ones would be deceived.

Matthew 24:24 LB

Lord, we pray that the Holy Spirit will always give us insight, so that we may be able to discern what is from the devil and not be caught in his trap.

David had conquered fear. That is why he could say that no man's heart need fail him because of Goliath. There was no panic; there was no feverish and wasteful excitement; there was no shouting to keep the spirits up. There was perfect calm.

For a child of God, fear is a conquered enemy. The power of the Holy Spirit gives us victory over fear. After Pentecost, we all stand on victory ground.

> . . . The Lord that delivered me . . . he will deliver me . . . .
>
> 1 Samuel 17:37

Make me, through Your Holy Spirit, a David who sees the Goliaths of today in the right proportions, Lord.

David conquered unbelief. He had a rich experience of the providential dealings of God, and his confidence was now unclouded and serene. He had known the Lord's power when he faced the bear and the lion and Goliath.

> . . . by my God have I leaped over a wall.
>
> 2 Samuel 22:30

Lord, help me to remember previous experiences which showed me Your victory. I know You never let me down.

September 14

The young champion of the Lord, David, won many victories before he faced Goliath. Everything depends on how I approach my supreme conflicts. If I am careless in small combats, I shall fail in the larger ones.

> What time I am afraid, I will trust in thee.
>
> Psalms 56:3

Lord, I must choose between fear and trust, unbelief and faith, defeat and victory. Yes, Lord, I will trust, believe, and conquer in Your power.

September 15

Do you think that any stone or obstacle on your path is there for no reason at all? Whether it be ugly, big, or small, you must believe that is has to be just where it is, but certainly not to hinder you from getting on, certainly not to weaken your courage and strength. A wise hand put it there, in order that you might take a good look at it and then talk about it with God, asking Him what He wants to make clear to you by it. And if you meet God at every stone, then every stone will bless you.

> These trials are only to test your faith, to see whether or not it is strong and pure . . . .
>
> 1 Peter 1:7 LB

Lord, it makes such a difference how I see my trials and problems. Show me what is the reason that I did not see things from Your point of view. Thank You, that You give me the right vision and the strength I need through Your Holy Spirit.

September 16

Whenever we are confronted with suffering, we immediately ask, "Why?" Might it not be that God wants to show us what *He* can do? Suffering drives us to our knees, and isn't that just where God wants us? Then His strength is most obvious. The Apostle Paul knew the value of being weak: God uses weak people.

> . . . my power is made perfect in weakness . . . .
>
> 2 Corinthians 12:9 RSV

Lord, make us willing to see suffering from Your side. Help us, so that our suffering, however great or small, may bring glory to You.

September 17

One of the reasons for suffering may be that it can bring out the best in others. And if we recognize this, we can praise God's goodness, for all the love and kindness one person shows to another ultimately comes from Him.

> Every good gift and every perfect gift is from above, and cometh down from the Father of lights . . . .
>
> James 1:17

Lord, please teach me to see Your love behind every expression of kindness and love that others show me.

September 18

Faith is a strong power, mastering any difficulty in the strength of the Lord who made heaven and earth.

> But they that wait upon the Lord shall renew their strength . . . they shall run, and not be weary; and they shall walk, and not faint.
>
> Isaiah 40:31

Lord, I am waiting upon You. Thank You that You are coming.

My book *Amazing Love* has been used by the Lord to show God's working in my life. Sometimes I experience that the enemy does not like some books. *Amazing Love,* originally written in Dutch, was translated into English, and I had only four copies of that translation. I was in Africa at the time, and sent one copy to the publisher in England. It never arrived.

I traveled to another country and heard that the first copy was lost, so I sent a second one. That one was also lost in the mail. I then sent a third copy, but they never received that one. I did not send the fourth one until I had four more copies made. This one arrived, and was published. It was reprinted many times.

> Love knows no limit to its endurance, no end to its trust, no fading of its hope; it can outlast anything. Love never fails.

> 1 Corinthians 13:7, 8 PHILLIPS

Thank You, Lord, that through Your Holy Spirit You make us channels of Your love.

In India an evangelist wanted to translate my book *Amazing Love* into his language. He gave it to a man who was a good translator. After a long time he asked when the translation would be ready. The man had lost it. He gave it to a second man, who became seriously ill. A third one was overtaken by a flood and so lost the copy. The evangelist himself had to flee for his life in the same flood, but was able to reach a little town. It was impossible to get away from there, because water surrounded the town. He used that time to translate the book himself, and so the enemy did not conquer.

And conspired all of them together . . . to hinder it.
Nevertheless we made our prayer unto our God . . . .

Nehemiah 4:8, 9

Thank You, Lord, that although the battle can be severe, with You,
we stand on victory ground.

September 21

You who are in much trouble can be of good cheer. One day your
troubles will be over and you will not need to fear anymore. Jesus
will give you victory. Therefore it is possible not to be over-
whelmed by difficulties. God will rejoice over you, and you will
rejoice in Him.

> . . . the Lord your God . . . . is a mighty Savior. He will give
> you victory . . . .

Zephaniah 3:17 LB

Lord, You have conquered all the power of the enemy, and You are
willing to make me victorious. I cannot understand this, but how I
thank You that it is true.

September 22

A woman once said, "Sometimes it seems that some canyons are
too wide for bridges. I pray I will have the courage to keep trying to
build them, anyway."

Difficulties can seem so impossible to overcome, but my father
taught us children that difficulties are there to *be* overcome.

> . . . without me ye can do nothing.

John 15:5

> I can do all things through Christ which strengtheneth me.

Philippians 4:13

I will tell You all the details of my problems and fears. Please,
Lord, use them as material to build a miracle.

September 23

If we find that victory is becoming hard—a matter of effort and of struggle—we are on the wrong track. We are not on God's basis. Faith does not struggle; faith lets God do it all.

Victory is not just an experience, not just a blessing (though it is that too); it is Jesus Christ Himself. Our victory lies in Him as a Person. Seeing "Jesus only" is victory.

> . . . in quietness and in confidence shall be your strength . . . .
>
> Isaiah 30:15

Time and again we think we have to do it in our own strength, and of course we fail, because we are not looking up to You, Lord Jesus, not trusting You. Remind us of Your Word at such times. We praise Your name that we can always put our confidence in You.

September 24

In a meeting, the pastor told the congregation that it was my birthday and that we had at that time a small work for orphans in Israel. In the collection box, a birthday card from a little boy was found. All the money he had saved to go and visit his aunt was stuck on the card "for the orphans." That was a wonderful birthday present!

Often I pray "Lord, protect me against unblessed money." I know that the Lord can do more with three blessed quarters than with a hundred unblessed dollars.

> Every man according as he purposeth in his heart, so let him give; not grudgingly, or of necessity: for God loveth a cheerful giver.
>
> 2 Corinthians 9:7

Make us cheerful givers, Lord, in order that You can bless what we give and there may be fruit for eternity.

September 25

Every gift—also money—begins to bear fruit *when we use it*. You must begin to discover the gifts God gave to you, and then you must open them up and use them, that others can be blessed through you.

> As every man hath received the gift, even so minister the same one to another, as good stewards of the manifold grace of God.
>
> 1 Peter 4:10

Open our eyes, Lord, to the gifts we received from You, and then please help us to use them in such a way that others may be blessed and give thanks to You.

September 26

If all things are possible with God, then all things are possible to him that believes in Him. Have you got any rivers you think are uncrossable?

> When you pass through the waters I will be with you; and through the rivers, they shall not overwhelm you . . . .
>
> Isaiah 43:2 RSV

Lord, I have no great faith, but I just look at Your promises in the Bible, and then I do not fear.

September 27

A compromise does not belong to the cross.

> . . . not my will, but thine, be done.
>
> Luke 22:42 RSV

Make me willing to be made willing to surrender all, Lord Jesus.

September 28

Slander is falsely accusing a person. It is taking away his good name and harming him. The Bible is very severe about slander.

> Him who slanders his neighbor secretly I will destroy . . . .
>
> Psalms 101:5 RSV

Lord, set a watch before my lips and help me not to talk about other people's faults and mistakes.

September 29

Gossip leads to criticism, and criticism kills love. We all know that. To be entangled in gossip is a snare and a delusion: It is love destroying, time killing, and a power that separates beyond recall. This is not God's will. We are called upon to do good, not to harm others.

> Withhold not good from them to whom it is due, when it is in the power of thine hand to do it.
>
> Proverbs 3:27

Father, how often we have let ourselves be entangled in the snare of gossip. Keep our eyes open to the danger when it comes near us. Teach us to be generous.

Our wonderful Saviour not only made provision that God's children might be delivered from the guilt of sin, but He also provided a clearly stated way whereby the shortcomings of those who are His might be confessed and forgiven and cleansed at any time. His Word also teaches that the obedient Christian may claim victory by faith, enter into a closer walk with God, fully surrender his life, and be filled with the Holy Spirit for whatever service in which he may be used.

> And their sins and iniquities will I remember no more . . . .
> Having therefore, brethren, boldness to enter into the holiest
> by the blood of Jesus . . . Let us draw near . . . .
>
> Hebrews 10:17, 19, 22

We praise You, Lord, that You provide the way—that You did all that had to be done, until You could say, "It is finished."

OCTOBER

October 1

A daily Prayer:

Oh, that mine eyes might closed be
to what concerns me not to see;
that deafness might possess mine ear
to what concerns me not to hear;
that truth my tongue might always tie
from ever speaking foolishly;
that no vain thought might ever rest
or be conceived within my breast;
that by each deed and word and thought
glory may to my God be brought.

But what are wishes? Lord, mine eye
on Thee is fixed, to Thee I cry.
Wash, Lord, and purify my heart,
and make it clean in every part.
And when it's clean, Lord, keep it too,
for that is more than I can do.

THOMAS ELLWOOD (1639)

Set a watch, O Lord, before my mouth; keep the door of my lips. Incline not my heart to any evil thing, to practise wicked works . . . .

Psalms 141:3, 4

Yes, Lord, You will have to do the work, but I must be willing to let You do it. Thank You for Your Spirit, who will always warn me when I am in danger of taking a wrong turn. Thank You, Lord, for Your victory.

October 2

Satan wastes no ammunition on those who are dead in trespasses and sins. Christians are far more strategic targets for him. Traveling all over the world, I saw Satan, with his timely shots, attacking Christians more than ever before. What a joy that we have so many promises in the Bible. We are holy, chosen, beloved, hidden in the hollow of His hand. We have a living Saviour, legions of angels. Count your many blessings!

. . . and having done all, to stand.

Ephesians 6:13

The devil is strong, much stronger than I. Thank You, Lord, that You are stronger, much stronger than the devil, and that with You I am more than conqueror. Hallelujah!

October 3

A discouraged person—you can pray for him. You can pray, "Open his eyes, that he may see his defense." You can pray like that if he is a Christian, when he has surrendered and knows how to use the Word of God. In that book, God's logistics are summed up.

If the discouraged person is not yet a Christian, pray, "Lord, lay Your hand on his eyes, that he sees that he must be born again and that he may then cast all his cares on You."

> . . . be of good cheer; I have overcome the world.
>
> John 16:33

Lord, You know that discouraged person I am concerned about better than I do. You love him. Show him that he may—must—surrender.

October 4

A great hindrance to Christians can be that they trust in orthodoxy and the sufficiency of their religious knowledge. When they sin and fail, they say, "If only we could be more earnest, more faithful."

The disciples needed not to be more earnest and faithful in using the privilege of having such a Master. More and more strenuous efforts would only have led to more and more bitter failures. They had to die to their old way of knowing Christ and receive the gift of an entirely new way of fellowship with Him.

> . . . worldly standards have ceased to count in our estimate of any man; even if once they counted in our understanding of Christ, they do so now no longer.
>
> 2 Corinthians 5:16 NEB

Lord, we pray that You remind us, each time we look at our failures, that we can never improve ourselves by trying in ourselves. Help us to let go of all worldly standards and receive the newness of life with a thankful heart.

October 5

There is only one right way of fighting sin. The secret of true overcoming is to calmly trust in the victory Jesus has already won for us, counting sin as dead, which it is, through Jesus' victory.

> So then, there remains a sabbath rest for the people of God; for whoever enters God's rest also ceases from his labors as God did from his.
>
> Hebrews 4:9, 10 RSV

Lord, You know how often I have tried and tried, without success. Thank You that Your Word says we can always fully trust You.

October 6

A king gave a little golden staff to his jester and said, "Keep this staff until you find a greater fool than you are, and then give it to him."

Later the jester came to the king, who was dying.

"I am going for a long journey to a country far away," said the king.

The jester said, "But I don't see any suitcases. Did you not make any preparations?"

"No," the king said, "I made neither reservations nor preparations."

Then the jester gave him the little staff and said, "Now I have found a greater fool than I!"

> . . . the foolishness of God is wiser than men; and the weakness of God is stronger than men.
>
> 1 Corinthians 1:25

Lord, I know that someday I will have to leave this world. Will You show me how to get ready?

October 7

We are never alone. We have His promise, and we need not be concerned. Through the power of the Holy Spirit, we can be used to glorify Jesus. Jesus is the door to a victorious life. Did you put your hand in His today? You must do it each new day. He loves you, and He wants to guide you. Look up to Him!

> For this God is our God for ever and ever: he will be our guide even unto death.
>
> Psalms 48:14

Lord Jesus, thank You that You are with us in every circumstance, in every trial, and that we need never be overcome if Your hand holds and leads us. Thank You that Your grace enfolds us.

October 8

When you come into a pitch-dark room, you cannot find out how things are. With your hands you can feel a chair, a table, a door, but the moment you put on the light switch, you suddenly see all the details.

Faith is the light that shows the reality of Jesus' victory and love. It is the Holy Spirit who gives us the faith.

And God said, Let there be light: and there was light.

Genesis 1:3

Lord, I have been in the dark. I did not see anything, but I felt something, and I surely felt unhappy. Make it light in me, that I can see things close and far away.

October 9

Where are you living? In the valley of your inadequacy or on the mountain of God's adequacy? Are you living in the valley of "I cannot," or are you on the hill of "God can?" Defeat is an abnormal experience. We must be more than conquerors.

> . . . I commend you to God, and to the word of his grace, which is able to build you up, and to give you an inheritance among all them which are sanctified.

Acts 20:32

Lord, thank You that when we are unable, You are able and willing to do the work through and for us.

October 10

In a Christian, the combinations of pride and Christianity, self-sufficiency and Christianity, irreconcilability and Christianity, backsliding and Christianity, are impossible. Jesus is very serious in His command to all decent and indecent sinners.

> . . . go, and sin no more.

John 8:11

Father, we pray that Your Spirit may enlighten our minds and show us every compromise we are making. Teach us how to live in Your light.

October 11

When you study the life of Jesus, you see again and again that He is Victor in every circumstance. Seeing a hungry crowd, He feeds them. Always He has the answer to people's problems. Three times He raised people from death. How was this possible? Because He was filled with the Holy Spirit—not *only* because He was the Son of God. For although He was the Son of God, yet He was also man and subject to hunger and temptation. But the Spirit caused Him to be victorious!

> He was faithful to him who appointed him . . . . Christ was faithful over God's house as a son . . . .
>
> Hebrews 3:2, 6 RSV

And, Lord, because the same Spirit works in us, we can also be faithful and victorious. Let us not hide behind false excuses.

October 12

When you overcome the dark powers, you become a strategic target for them, so you must know how to remain on victory ground. Remember that with Jesus you are more than conqueror. When they attack, pray for the protection of Jesus' blood. Don't wait until you understand that; just obey.

> And they overcame him by the blood of the Lamb, and by the word of their testimony . . . .
>
> Revelation 12:11

Teach me, Holy Spirit, how to fight victoriously in Jesus' power.

October 13

Because of listening to the enemy, Satan, who is the accuser of the saints day and night, we see ourselves as slaves and prisoners of sin—without hope. But the door is open. Come out, enter into freedom.

> I am the door .
>
> John 10:7

Thank You, Jesus, that I may lay my hand in Yours and that You set me free. Hallelujah!

October 14

Into the heart of every believer comes an intense longing for victory over sin and power for service. It is inconceivable that the Lord of a perfect salvation should not make provision for every need of His children. There must be a way to purity and power. But how few avail themselves of Jesus' promise:

> He who believes in me . . . Out of his heart shall flow rivers of living water.
>
> John 7:38 RSV

Lord, I believe in You. Fulfill my longing for a life in Your strength.

October 15

It is a trick of the deceiver to make us think that we are still sinning when we have met all God's conditions for confessing sin and claiming the fulness of the Holy Spirit.

God's faithfulness and truth are the guarantees of our forgiveness, once the blood of Jesus Christ cleanses us from all the sins we confess. His blood will never cleanse an excuse. We must fully surrender.

> to open their eyes and turn them from darkness to light, and from the power of Satan to God, so that they may receive forgiveness of sins . . . .
>
> Acts 26:18 NIV

Thank You, Father, that You made it possible for us to be delivered from the power of Satan and to receive forgiveness of sins. May our lives prove the truth of this fact. We pray that those who do not know You yet may be drawn to You.

October 16

Is there any purpose in feeling guilty? There is. The purpose of guilt is to bring us to Jesus. That is what any feeling of guilt should do for you.

> If our conscience condemns us, we know that God is greater than our conscience and that he knows everything.
>
> 1 John 3:20 TEV

O Lord, thank You that You also called me. Thank You that I can bring all my feelings of guilt to You. Thank You for cleansing me.

Don't build a ladder of good works in order to reach heaven. Heaven is a long distance away from "good people." But it is only one step from a sinner.

. . . I came not to call the righteous, but sinners.

Mark 2:17 RSV

Lord Jesus, thank You that I can come to You, because You are calling sinners such as me. Thank You for Your great love.

October 18

Jesus died in our stead, that we might receive forgiveness. He lives that we might know deliverance. I need forgiveness for my sins. I need deliverance from the power of my sins. God's Spirit can give me both.

For God hath . . . given us the spirit . . . of power . . . .

2 Timothy 1:7

Lord, how You must love me that You were willing to die even for me.

October 19

People sometimes say they have committed a sin so bad that they cannot bring it to God, or that He cannot forgive and forget. But there is no sin too great to bring to Jesus. Those who come to Him, He will never cast out. The first step is to come to Jesus and to turn away from sin, in His strength. Then we shall be cleansed and sanctified.

For this is the will of God, your sanctification . . . .

1 Thessalonians 4:3 RSV

I need Your help, Lord, to turn away from sin. Thank You that in Your strength I can. I long to be sanctified.

October 20

Since Satan attacks us so often, it is necessary to confess often. Regardless of how old people may be, or how long they have ministered in the name of Jesus Christ, they still need to confess their sins again and again, and ask forgiveness.

When we follow Jesus, He makes us sensitive to the smallest sin that comes between Him and us. Whenever this happens, we can go to Him at once to confess this sin.

If we confess our sins, he . . . will forgive our sins . . . .

1 John 1:9 RSV

Lord, make us increasingly sensitive to anything that tries to come between You and us. Thank You that whenever this happens, we can go to You and tell You all about it. Thank You that You will always forgive.

October 21

The devil accuses us night and day. He likes to discourage us, because then we cannot be strong. But the Word of God says to us, over and over again, "Be strong in the Lord." The Lord can give us this command because He Himself gives us His strength.

As soon as we realize that there is a sin in our hearts, we must bring it to the Lord, because that sin makes us insecure and weak. ". . . your sins have hid his face from you . . ." (Isaiah 59:2). But when we confess our sins, He will forgive us and make His face to shine upon us anew. We must *know* that it is really true that:

> . . . the blood of Jesus his Son cleanses us from all sin.
>
> 1 John 1:7 RSV

Father, teach us more and more the wonderful power of Jesus' blood.

October 22

Theology wants to know where sin comes from. Jesus tells us how we can get rid of sin. We shall not conquer the world with theology. Knowing that Jesus conquered sin and all the power of the devil when He died on the cross will make us conquerors.

> For whatsoever is born of God overcometh the world: and this is the victory that overcometh the world, even our faith. Who is he that overcometh the world, but he that believeth that Jesus is the Son of God?
>
> 1 John 5:4, 5

O Lord, we thank You that it is possible to live a victorious life, because we know and believe that You are the Son of God and that You are Victor!

158

Those who come to Christ must have the right attitude. They must know they need salvation because they are sinners. Only the Holy Spirit convicts of sin. And we have only to deal with our own sins, not with those of others.

> Search me, O God, and know my heart; test my thoughts. Point out anything you find in me that makes you sad, and lead me along the path of everlasting life.
>
> Psalms 139:23, 24 LB

Father, I also pray that You will search my heart and show me if there is anything that has caused me not to walk in Your way. You know my thoughts, even those I want to hide. Make me willing for Your Spirit to work in me.

October 24

We must have clear vision, but our sins often hinder us. They confuse our sight. He who waits for Jesus' coming again should be sensitive to every shadow that comes between his Master and himself, and he should not rest until his vision is clear again. We must clearly understand that this does not mean striving to make ourselves better and better. We must look at Jesus, our hope. He is the Lord who sanctifies us. The Holy Spirit gives us all we need.

> The Spirit . . . produces in human life fruits such as these: love, joy, peace, patience, kindness, generosity, fidelity, tolerance and self-control . . . .
>
> Galatians 5:22, 23 PHILLIPS

Thank You, Lord, that You sanctify us. Thank You for Your Holy Spirit, who not only gives us what we need, but who also produces fruit in our lives that is well pleasing to You.

October 25

When Jesus is in your heart, you suddenly see all unconfessed sins so clearly. Together with Him, there comes a spring cleaning in your heart that sets you free, takes away the guilt, and gives you vision.

> Draw nigh unto my soul, and redeem it . . . .
>
> Psalms 69:18

Thank You, Lord Jesus, that You are willing to live in *my* heart. What a miracle! *You in my heart!*

October 26

How often we must pray, "Have mercy upon me, O God, according to thy lovingkindness: according unto the multitude of thy tender mercies blot out my transgressions" (Psalms 51:1). But then we can add:

> Restore unto me the joy of thy salvation . . . .
>
> Psalms 51:12

O Father, how great are Your love and mercy. How we thank You for blotting out our transgressions and for restoring unto us the joy of Your salvation.

God has let us share His secrets. We know about it because God has sent His Spirit to tell us, and His Spirit searches and shows us God's deepest secrets.

> . . . Eye hath not seen, nor ear heard, neither have entered into the heart of man, the things which God hath prepared for them that love him.
>
> 1 Corinthians 2:9

Our Father, how You must love us, that You are willing to let us share the things that are hidden from those who do not love You. Help us not to brush such love aside.

God never takes away; God gives. If I reach out and take someone for myself and the Lord steps in between, that does not mean God takes. It rather means that He is asking me to turn my back on something or someone I should not have, because He has a far greater purpose for my life.

> . . . behold with thine eyes, and hear with thine ears, and set thine heart upon all that I shall shew thee; for to the intent that I might shew them unto thee art thou brought hither. . . .
>
> Ezekiel 40:4

Father, thank You that You have a purpose for my life. I trust You to work it out, and because You love me, I know that You will only do that which is to Your glory.

October 29

God's fulness is available when we serve Him.

> But you shall receive power . . . you shall be my witnesses . . . .

> Acts 1:8 RSV

Thank You, Lord, for this promise. Help us to be faithful witnesses, filled with Your very power.

October 30

Don't look at the people who do you wrong. It is God who allows you to bear this difficulty. If you are in the center of the will of God, you can accept that all comes from His dear hand.

> Strengthened with all might, according to his glorious power, unto all patience and longsuffering with joyfulness.

> Colossians 1:11

Holy Spirit, turn my eyes away from myself, from other people, from my problems, and straight to Jesus.

God will give us the state of life which is best for us. And because He is the Lord of our lives, we can thank Him for whatever He gives, whether it is marriage and a family or remaining single. He alone knows in which state of life we can best serve Him. And is not that our heart's desire?

Those God calls to live single lives are always happy in that state. It is a special gift. This happiness, this contentment, is the evidence of God's plan.

> . . . our heart shall rejoice in him, because we have trusted in his holy name.
>
> Psalms 33:21

Help us to share with others the joy You gave to us, Father. We know You are guiding our lives according to Your will, giving us Your peace. Let others
stances in

NOVEMBER

November 1

When a part of the body is injured, the pain causes tensions, and tensions in their turn cause pain. It is the same with anger and resentment. A good bath of forgiveness makes us ready for peace and joy. But if we give ourselves over to hatred and resentment, we will receive the opposite of peace and joy.

> for the anger of man does not work the righteousness of God.
>
> James 1:20 RSV

Your love for those
love.

And their sins and iniquities will I remember no more.

Hebrews 10:17

How great Your love is, heavenly Father, that for Christ's sake You will not remember our sins!

November 3

Heaven is a prepared place for prepared people. Theology in the hands of the Holy Spirit is a beautiful science, but in the hands of unbelievers, it is death. Listen to the simple faith of those who read only the Bible and trust only in God. They don't care if some theologian says that heaven is a fable. Those who have found Jesus, know that heaven does exist.

. . . I go to prepare a place for you.

John 14:2

How wonderful, Lord, that You went to prepare a place for me. Help me to live in such a way that, when my time comes to go to that place, I shall be fully prepared.

November 4

Have you ever thought of the fact that one day we shall all have to appear before God and then asked yourself, "But who will be able to stand? What about my sins?"

It is true: Sin has to be dealt with before we can come to God and have fellowship with Him. But God *did* deal with sin. His Son Jesus Christ gave His life as a ransom, and God made a new covenant based on His own faithfulness.

For I will be merciful to their unrighteousness, and their sins and their iniquities will I remember no more.

Hebrews 8:12

Father, I thank You for Your promise. I thank You that You will do it, because Your Word says that You will not lie or repent of what You said.

November 5

Have you been born again? It is so important. When a child is born, there is great joy for the parents. The baby does a lot of crying, but we, who know what it means to live, say, "Baby, why cry? You were born, and you received a life to live."

Jesus told Nicodemus how important it is to be born again and to receive another life: eternal life. He said:

> . . . Except a man be born again, he cannot see the kingdom of God.

> John 3:3

We thank You, Lord that when we come to You, accepting You as our Lord and Saviour, we shall be born again and receive eternal life.

November 6

Have you accepted Jesus as your Saviour? That is a great experience. Yet, when one is converted and says yes to Jesus, it does not mean the end of a new experience, but the beginning. You have entered the gate to a new life. You will find complete joy and liberty there. Don't be too concerned about what Christians should and should not do. You can leave those things safely to the Holy Spirit to show you, for you have not been brought to a religion or doctrine, but to a Person: Jesus Christ.

> . . . now, in Christ Jesus, you who were once far off are brought near through the shedding of Christ's blood.

> Ephesians 2:13 PHILLIPS

Thank You, Lord, that the power of Your blood is still the same and that it continues to cleanse and protect each one who comes to You.

November 7

There are Christians who have yet to learn that Jesus stands outside the door of their hearts. Are you a Christian? Is Jesus in your heart? He knocks. Let Him in!

> Behold, I stand at the door, and knock: if any man hear my voice, and open the door, I will come in to him . . . .
>
> Revelation 3:20

Yes, Lord, come in and have fellowship with me. I see that I was satisfied much too soon. Really come into my heart, so that we can sup together. What a joy!

November 8

Often people think that working for the Lord, as a missionary or a pastor or an evangelist, is a matter of ability. Because they have no special gifts in that respect, they think they cannot do anything. But working for the Lord is far more a matter of *availability,* and we are all called to take our share. God gave a gift to each one of us. It is our responsibility to make it available to Him. One thing every child of God can do is pray. However weak or young or old we are, we can always pray. And it might well be that prayer is, in God's eyes, the most important thing.

> Pray without ceasing.
>
> 1 Thessalonians 5:17

Lord, we do not know how to pray or what to ask for. Teach us to pray and make us faithful, so that we can do our part in serving You.

Prayer is sanctified by the name of Jesus. Therefore use this name! It is the most powerful name in heaven or on earth.

> . . . if you ask the Father for anything in my name, he will give it you. So far you have asked nothing in my name . . . .
>
> John 16:23, 24 NEB

Lord Jesus, it is true I cannot come to the Father with anything of myself. You told us that we can always go to Him in Your name. How I thank You for this!

Looking unto Jesus in prayer is a blessed training. Prayer without listening is like going to a person, asking questions, and leaving without waiting for an answer.

We need some practice. We have prayed so much without listening that we do not always hear the answer immediately. Then we must wait upon the Lord. This waiting upon Him is a blessing in itself.

> . . . they that wait upon the Lord shall renew their strength . . . .
>
> Isaiah 40:31 LB

Lord, teach me to pray and teach me to listen and understand Your sometimes still, small voice.

November 11

The enemy considers it most important to destroy our prayer life by little faith, lack of time, and doubt. We should know that prayerlessness is sin for a child of God. But we can confess this sin and be cleansed.

> . . . I said, I will confess my transgressions unto the Lord; and thou forgavest the iniquity of my sin . . . .
>
> Psalms 32:5

Lord, thank You for Your faithfulness. Thank You for forgiveness and cleansing. Make us always willing to confess.

November 12

Prayerlessness is a sin. It is a creeping paralysis, beginning with neglect of prayer and ending in utter prayerlessness. By neglecting prayer, a Christian becomes prey to a hundred voices.

> . . . ye shall go and pray unto me, and I will hearken unto you.
>
> Jeremiah 29:12

Father, forgive me for not keeping in constant touch with You and for letting other things take up my mind and draw me away from You. How great is Your mercy, that I may go to You again and that You will listen to me.

November 13

Are your prayers unanswered? You must be convinced that your loving Father hears whenever one of His children makes any request. God does not always grant what we ask, because He knows what we don't know. He sees His side all the time; one day we shall see it, too.

> And we know that all that happens to us is working for our good if we love God . . . .
>
> Romans 8:28 LB

Father, I thank You for every answered and every unanswered prayer.

November 14

During a time when I was unable to do what I wanted so much to do, I was very conscious of my inability. Yet I knew that the Lord would go on with His work, and I could thank Him for this.

One evening, these two thoughts kept coming to me:"Tomorrow I must get on further," and "Tomorrow I shall be permitted to get on." What a comfort to see God's side of the matter once again!

> . . . who began a good work in you will bring it to completion at the day of Jesus Christ.
>
> Philippians 1:6 RSV

Lord, keep us from thinking we have reached the goal. Make us willing to have our hearts searched by You. Let not past and present difficulties close us in, but let us continue on our path in the power of Your Spirit.

November 15

Do you witness for the Lord? I do not find any word in the Bible for so-called *secret believers*.

> What I tell you in the dark, utter in the light; and what you hear whispered, proclaim upon the housetops. And do not fear those who kill the body but cannot kill the soul . . . .
>
> Matthew 10:27, 28 RSV

Forgive me, Lord, that I was afraid to witness. Make me, through Your fulness, more than conqueror.

November 16

It is not important how much can I do for Jesus, but how much Jesus can do through me.

> . . . I will make you to become fishers of men.
>
> Mark 1:17

Lord, how I need to look to You, and not to myself. Turn my eyes, through the Holy Spirit, in the right direction.

November 17

Many communists are articulate, while many Christians are tongue-tied, like the mouth of the MacKenzie River, which is frozen over three-quarters of the year.

It may be true ''that the devil is dead and gone, but sensible people would like to know who carries the business on.'' But he is a conquered enemy, since Jesus came to destroy the work of the devil. We overcome through the blood of the Lamb and the name of Jesus. Those who are with us are more and stronger than those who are against us. At our side are a powerful high priest and legions of angels.

> . . . because . . . [Jesus] has suffered and been tempted, he is able to help those who are tempted.
>
> Hebrews 2:18 RSV

Lord, through the Holy Spirit make me an articulate, joyful witness for You.

November 18

Soul winning is a task and a privilege from which no believer is exempt. Witnessing for Christ is the greatest work in the world. It is the work that is most honoring to Christ, most joyful to the believer, most beneficial in its blessed effects to those who are won.

> . . . Go . . . preach the gospel . . . .
>
> Mark 16:15

Make me sensitive, Lord, to the needs of those whom I meet, that I may know when to speak to them of You, that they may come to know You personally.

November 19

The best way of reaching others is to say, as simply as possible, "I was blind. Now I can see."

> The Lord openeth the eyes of the blind . . .
>
> Psalms 146:8

I praise You, Lord, that You opened my blind eyes, and that now I can see. May others see the change in my life and be drawn to You.

The Gospel is not a secret to be hoarded, but a story to be heralded. Are you saved? Do you think that is what matters most? If so, what about those you meet every day? Do you keep it all to yourself, or do you do what the shepherds at Bethlehem did when the angel brought them the tidings of great joy?

> . . . as for you, go and proclaim the kingdom of God.
>
> Luke 9:60 RSV

Forgive me, Lord, if I think I can keep the good news of salvation to myself. Show me to whom I must pass it on today.

November 21

The only evidence of the truth of the Bible that is seen by thousands today is the men and women who claim to be Christians. Are you and I proof of the Bible's truth?

> Do all you have to do without grumbling or arguing, so that you may be blameless and harmless, faultless children of God . . . shining like lights in a dark world. For you hold up in your hands the very word of life.
>
> Philippians 2:14–16 PHILLIPS

O Lord, make us to be men and women who do all they have to do with a willing and cheerful heart, that those who do not know You yet may long to be Yours.

The world does not read the Bible, but it reads you and me. Does it see you grow like Peter, glow like Stephen, go like Paul? If not, ask God to make you a person in whom the world can see what He can do with a yielded life.

> Not that we are sufficient of ourselves to think any thing as of ourselves; but our sufficiency is of God.
>
> 2 Corinthians 3:5

Father, thank You that we need not force ourselves to be and do something special. Thank You that You will do that in us which is pleasing to You. Make us willing to let You do whatever You think necessary.

November 23

We are called to be God's ambassadors, His missionaries, the light of the world in a time of chaos and great darkness. And as we see chaos and darkness increasing, our responsibility also increases.

> . . . : we are ambassadors for Christ, God making his appeal through us. We beseech you on behalf of Christ, be reconciled to God.
>
> 2 Corinthians 5:20 RSV

Lord Jesus, help us to remain watching and praying, that we may be able to discern other people's needs and go and help them, pointing them to You.

What is God doing with people who never hear the Gospel? What are you doing with them? How will the heathen be saved, when they never hear the message of God's love? Will you perhaps have to bring it to them?

> But how shall they ask him to save them unless they believe in him? And how can they believe in him if they have never heard about him? And how can they hear about him unless someone tells them?
>
> Romans 10:14 LB

Lord, show me whether You want me to be such a preacher. If not, show me what You do want me to do.

November 25

When Jesus told His disciples where they were to go to preach the Gospel, He said they were to go to the utmost parts of the earth. That really meant they had to surrender their own will. Jerusalem was hostile to them. Samaria was their natural enemy. Of themselves, they did not want to go. But the fact that Jesus sent them made all the difference. Now they were safe and secure.

> . . . now then, whatsoever God hath said unto thee, do.
>
> Genesis 31:16

Lord, give me an attentive ear, that I can hear what You are saying, that I may do what You tell me to do.

When we are ready to witness, we are also ready to suffer. What about you? Are you ready to tell everyone who is willing to listen? It is settled for all eternity that Jesus is Victor. The whole world belongs to Him!

> . . . thanks be to God, who gives us the victory through our Lord Jesus Christ.
>
> 1 Corinthians 15:57 RSV

Father, make us aware of the needs of those we meet, that we may minister to them, telling them the glad news of Your great love in giving Your only Son for us.

November 27

We need heroes and heroines for Christ, people eager to go out and preach Christ to those who have not yet heard of Him. We need men willing to point them to Jesus, the Saviour of all mankind.

> . . . all shall know me, from the least to the greatest.
>
> Hebrews 8:11

Lord, we pray for men and women who are willing to bring the Gospel to those who have not yet heard it. Tell me what You want me to do.

November 28

The multitudes are waiting for the workers. Will the workers come? Or will they have to go on waiting until it is too late and they have to cry out, as they go into eternity, "The harvest is past and we are not saved."?

> . . . how are they to believe in him of whom they have never heard? . . .
>
> Romans 10:14 RSV

Again, Lord, I pray: Show me what You want me to do.

November 29

It is not my ability, but my response to His ability, that counts. It is not what happens to me that matters, but what I do with what happens to me.

> . . . who is sufficient for these things?
>
> 2 Corinthians 2:16

> . . . our sufficiency is of God.
>
> 2 Corinthians 3:5

Father, thank You that You are the All-Sufficient One and that I can always depend on Your ability.

November 30

I stand amazed at the unfathomable complexity of God's wisdom and God's knowledge. How can man ever understand His reasons for His doings, or explain His methods of working?

> . . . who hath known the mind of the Lord? or who hath been his counsellor?
>
> Romans 11:34

O Lord, how great You are! I can only bow down and worship You for Your majesty and wisdom.

DECEMBER

December 1

Man has to go through many experiences in order to receive the spiritual vision which is needed to see the divine plan. Some experiences are hard. But then nothing that is of great value is easily obtained. If we let God do the work, He will show us His plan little by little. One day we shall see it all. When we feel as if there is nothing but darkness around us, let us not forget that a film has to be developed in a darkroom in order to bring out the beauty.

Where there is no vision, the people perish . . . .
Proverbs 29:18

Father, keep us close to Yourself, that in times of darkness and difficulties we may feel Your presence. Thank You that one day we shall see the whole plan You have for our lives.

December 2

Sooner or later, to most who follow Christ, there comes a time when flesh and heart fail. Feelings and fears can be like a torrent of rough water, and we see no way to cross it. The words *But God* make all the difference then.

AMY CARMICHAEL

My flesh and my heart faileth: but God is the strength of my heart, and my portion for ever.

Psalms 73:26

Father, You know that at times we have no strength whatever. Help us then to turn to You. With You, there is plenty for everyone.

December 3

There are two great forces at work in the world today: the unlimited power of God and the limited power of Satan. So when we have surrendered our lives and hearts to Jesus Christ, we need never be overcome.

. . . strengthened with all power, according to his glorious might, for all endurance and patience with joy.

Colossians 1:11 RSV

Thank You, Father, that Your glorious power will strengthen us whenever we need it. And You know how much we need it, just to be patient and longsuffering with joyfulness.

December 4

To grow spiritually, we must recognize that every part of us belongs to God, once we have accepted Jesus Christ as Lord and Saviour. When we are totally emptied of ourselves, we can be full of the Holy Spirit. Then we shall be conquerors and able to accept all things from His hand.

Haven't you yet learned that your body is the home of the Holy Spirit God gave you, and that he lives within you? Your own body does not belong to you. For God has bought you with a great price. So use every part of your body to give glory back to God, because he owns it.

1 Corinthians 6:19, 20 LB

Lord, we must confess that we have not yet fully learned that our body does not belong to us. Help us, that we may glorify You by the way we live.

December 5

The things of this world are empty in themselves, and so are many of our ambitions, because they are earthbound. Jesus made us children of God, our Father who is in heaven, and so He wants us to be heavenly minded.

. . . that ye might be filled with the knowledge of his will in all wisdom and spiritual understanding.

Colossians 1:9

Lord, we pray that we may know Your will and grow spiritually, so that we may bring joy to our heavenly Father's heart.

December 6

In our days, man and his achievements are increasingly being brought into the center of people's thinking. This may seem to be the right thing, because man has indeed achieved much. However, if we really think man is on top of everything, we make a mistake. We forget that all man's thinking is nothing but afterthought, copying what God has originally thought long, long ago.

. . . by him were all things created, that are in heaven, and that are in earth, visible and invisible . . . all things were created by him, and for him.

Colossians 1:16

Lord, we worship You. We thank You that we know You are the Omnipotent One and that all things are in You.

December 7

It is sometimes hard to reconcile the Christian's dual role of being separate from the world and yet part of it. We are *in* the world, but not *of* the world, and we must learn to discern between the two. When we realize what it means that we are not *of* the world, we begin to learn the secret of living in it as we should, being more willing to serve God in all circumstances, more willing to serve those around us and give to them out of the vast riches we possess in Christ.

> And my God will supply every need of yours according to his riches in glory in Christ Jesus.
>
> Philippians 4:19 RSV

O Father, how we thank You that whenever we need anything, You will give it to us. Also we thank You for this wonderful promise in Your Word, which covers each and every need.

December 8

In order to grow in our faith, we need to be placed into circumstances where we are forced to reach out to the Source of our strength. That is the way our spiritual vision is exercised, and how we discover new dimensions in our God.

> . . . all my springs are in thee.
>
> Psalms 87:7

Father, I can say with the psalmist that it is good for me to draw near to You. Renew my strength, for You are the Source from which I live. And then help me to tell others.

December 9

God's will is not a hidden mystery that you must set out to discover. You must simply open your heart to the evident will of God. Remember that God wants you to know His will and that He is doing everything He can to make it obvious to you.

> . . do not be foolish, but understand what the will of the Lord is
>
> Ephesians 5:17 RSV

Our Father, I thank You that it is so simple to know what Your will is and that You Yourself make it known to me. Cause me to fully understand.

December 10

We have to conquer the world in us and the world around us. In the inner world there is pride, selfishness, guilt, bitterness, greed. All these things must be conquered. We ourselves can never do this.

> . . . with us is the Lord our God to help us, and to fight our battles . . . .
>
> 2 Chronicles 32:8

Thank You, Lord, that You will always strengthen us and make us victorious.

Are you acting as if your life were your own? You lost the right to do so on Calvary. Christ bought you—lock, stock, and barrel. What does He get from you in return?

> Live as obedient children before God. Don't let your character be moulded by the desires of your ignorant days, but be holy in every part of your lives . . . .
>
> 1 Peter 1:14, 15 PHILLIPS

You alone can enable us, O Lord, to live a completely surrendered life. Help us, we pray, that our lives may show what You can do.

December 12

Let us not forget that we are eternity people. We are citizens of heaven; our outlook goes beyond this world.

> . . . take heed to yourselves, lest at any time your hearts be overcharged with . . . cares of this life . . . .
>
> Luke 21:34

Thank You, Lord, that You have given me eternal life. Let Your heavenly light shine on my life of today, so I see things in the right perspective.

December 13

It is never a waste of time to look unto the Lord. Looking is a most-needed part of our daily discipline.

> And what I say unto you I say unto all, Watch.
>
> Mark 13:37

Forgive me, Lord, for looking in the wrong direction. I know that is the reason I was discouraged.

December 14

Elijah prayed to God for his servant: "Open his eyes that he may see." What was there to see? A great army to defend them.

We may pray for others, that their eyes may be opened, and also for ourselves. It is the Holy Spirit who does the job. Jesus said we would have power when the Holy Spirit came upon us, and that is because the Holy Spirit gives us vision.

> . . . when he, the Spirit of truth, is come, he will guide you into all truth . . . .
>
> John 16:13

Lord, what a victory when we see Your way, Your plan.

December 15

An unsanctified Christian is not in the will of God. He is a burden and a sorrow to God. The Father wants His child to be sanctified.

> . . . as he who called you is holy, be holy yourselves in all your conduct; since it is written, "You shall be holy, for I am holy."
>
> 1 Peter 1:15, 16 RSV

Lord, whenever You command me to do anything, You also give me the power to fulfill it. I thank You for that.

December 16

How much more we know than those for whom Christmas only means the ringing of bells and Father Christmas, or the many who only prepare for Christmas by posting their Christmas cards in time and wrapping their presents! They do their best to do their duty every year, because it is a yearly ritual for them and they are afraid people might think that they forgot them.

Those who know Jesus Christ have received what the Bible calls an inexpressible gift. Is He the center of your Christmas?

> The Lord looked down from heaven upon the children of men,
> to see if there were any that did understand, and seek God.

Psalms 14:2

Lord, Your Holy Spirit can give us this understanding. We pray You, let Your Spirit work in us more and more, enlightening our understanding so that others may find the Way of life because of what they see in us.

December 17

The one aim of the call of God is the satisfaction of God, not the call to do something for Him. We are not sent to battle for God, but to be used by God in His battles. Are we being more devoted to service than to Jesus Christ?

> . . . Lord; thou knowest that I love thee. He [Jesus] saith
> unto him, Feed my lambs.

John 21:15

O Lord, I love You, and that is why I am so glad when You use me. Give me discernment.

December 18

Sanctification is not a heavy yoke, but a joyful liberation. If you have surrendered to Jesus Christ, He will work this liberation in you.

> . . . Christ Jesus, who of God is made unto us . . . sanctifi-
> cation . . . .

1 Corinthians 1:30

Thank You, Father, that whatever You command us, You made possible through Jesus Christ, Your Son.

December 19

Someone asked Henrietta Mears, the week before she died, "If you should have an opportunity to live your life again, which things would you do differently?"

Her answer was, "I would trust Jesus more than I have done this time."

. . . in quietness and confidence is your strength . . . .

Isaiah 30:15 LB

Lord, increase my trust by Your Holy Spirit.

December 20

Sanctification brings us to a new battlefield: that of the spirit. The devil tries to keep us concerned with our own selves—preaching self, looking at self, looking at our own faith, looking at our own experiences—and he says, "Rest on those experiences."

Are you so foolish? Having begun with the Spirit, are you now ending with the flesh?

Galatians 3:3 RSV

Lord, I know that in my own strength I never can accomplish the things of Your Kingdom. But thank You that in Your strength I can.

December 21

We rob the work of Jesus of its efficacy, and we stand powerless before the adversary, when we doubt the integrity of the Word of God. There is no other way of proving the authenticity of the Bible but by believing it and by living it ourselves.

> The Son is the radiance of God's glory and the exact representation of his being, sustaining all things by his powerful word . . . .
>
> Hebrews 1:3 NIV

We thank You, Lord, that Your power is available to us, if only we depend on You. Use us so others see that You are the only wise God.

December 22

Christmas is no duty! The coming of Jesus was a free gift to us all. Christmas reminds us of the fact that He came as a baby. Let us prepare our hearts for that celebration, in order to be able to prepare others for it.

> Then said I, Lo, I come . . . I delight to do thy will, O my God . . . .
>
> Psalms 40:7, 8

Lord, we thank You that You were willing to come to this earth with such a desire to do Your Father's will. Make us willing for whatever You may ask from us.

December 23

We must crawl before we walk, and we must walk before we run This is the natural development in the life of us all. Actually, it applies to all spheres of life. Never run ahead of yourself; you'll never make it. Another thing is that we must *learn* to crawl and to walk and to run—and for this we need the help of others. The Bible also speaks of this when it tells how God taught His people

> I taught Ephraim also to go, taking them by their arms . . . .
>
> Hosea 11:3

Heavenly Father, thank You that You are helping us, leading us, teaching us in the small details of everyday life. Make us willing to obey, not trying to do things in our own limited strength, waiting for Your timing in our development.

December 24

We are God's children if we have accepted Jesus Christ as our Lord and Saviour. If only we knew how truly we belong to Him, everything would be so different. God is continually remembering us; and if He claims our life for Himself, it is because we share the same life of eternity.

> See what love the Father has given us, that we should be called children of God; and so we are . . . .
>
> 1 John 3:1 RSV

Father, we bow down before You and worship You. It is beyond our understanding that You love us so much.

God made a little opening in the sky to show the shepherds a little bit of heaven. He will show you still greater joy if you open your heart for the fulness of the Holy Spirit. Even now, your eyes may see some of the far vast reaches of eternity.

> . . . we all . . . are changed into the same image from glory to glory even as by the Spirit of the Lord.
>
> 2 Corinthians 3:18

I would like to see much now, Lord. Will You, by Your Holy Spirit, open my eyes? Thank You.

December 26

Jesus not only wants to save us from our sins—He wants to restore God's image in us. We never can love like this, but it is not necessary. When we put our weak hand into the strong hand of the Lord, then He will do it. He Himself causes His love to overflow. Just imagine—unblamable in holiness! This we can never achieve by trying. But *He* can!

> And the very God of peace sanctify you wholly; and I pray God your whole spirit and soul and body be preserved blameless unto the coming of our Lord Jesus Christ.
>
> 1 Thessalonians 5:23

Our Father, we worship You. You are the Almighty One, and You will do that in us which we in ourselves never can do. Thank You for the greatness of Your power.

189

How is it possible to be blameless—holy? When we look at ourselves, such words just frighten us. But when we look unto the Lord, we never need be afraid, for verse 24 in 1 Thessalonians 5 says: "Faithful is he that calleth you, who also will do it."

We can rely on these words, because we know that on the Cross of Calvary all was finished that had to be done to prepare us for the future. Jesus said: "It is finished." And when we look at Calvary's cross, we know: Faithful is He who did it and who also will do it. It is Jesus who calls us.

> I came not to call the righteous, but sinners to repentance.
>
> Luke 5:32

Lord, we thank You that *You* are calling us. You know how weak we feel in ourselves, how we never can become blameless and holy by trying. But, oh, we thank You that You did all that had to be done and that we just can accept it from You.

Will God be defeated? No! After the period of darkness, His trumpet will sound, and His Son Jesus Christ will come. Then it will be very clearly manifested that the Gospel has indeed been brought to all nations.

> One word of command, one shout from the archangel, one blast from the trumpet of God and the Lord himself will come down from Heaven! Those who have died in Christ will be the first to rise, and then we who are still living will be swept up with them into the clouds to meet the Lord in the air. And after that we shall be with him for ever.
>
> 1 Thessalonians 4:16, 17 PHILLIPS

What a wonderful future lies before us, Lord. We are looking to the day of Your coming. Help us encourage one another again and again.

December 29

What a joy to know Him, the Lord Jesus Christ, who was born at Bethlehem, who died on the cross for our sins, who was raised, and who is with us always, until the end of the world!

Let us do what the shepherds did—tell it to everyone who is willing to listen.

> He who did not spare his own Son but gave him up for us all,
> will he not also give us all things with him?
>
> Romans 8:32 RSV

Our Father, we can only thank You for Your great gift in Jesus Christ, Your Son, by passing on these good tidings of great joy to others.

December 30

The certain hope of every child of God is that death is not the end, but only the gate to greater life. This keeps believers from fearing death. If we gave our heart to Jesus, we can be certain that He prepared a place for us in His Father's house.

Death is not a pit, but a tunnel leading to a far greater fulness of light than we ever saw before, because we shall then be in the light of God.

> For I know that my redeemer liveth, and that he shall stand at
> the latter day upon the earth: And . . . in my flesh shall I see
> God.
>
> Job 19:25, 26

Lord, how I long for the day when I shall see You and shall no longer need the light of the sun or of a lamp, because You shall give me Your light.

This year brought us closer to the great end battle and to the return of the Lord Jesus. May He use you and me to hasten this return, because when the last of the Gentiles has turned to Jesus, the time will have come. You and I could be used to bring this last one to Him. What a joy!

> . . . like unto men that wait for their lord, when he will return . . . Blessed are those servants, whom the lord when he cometh, shall find watching . . . .
>
> Luke 12:36, 37

Lord, show me if there is a compromise in my surrender, whether that is the reason I do not enjoy the fruit of the Spirit more fully. Lord, use me to build Your Kingdom.